THE REPLACED APOSTLE

How the devil derailed
the church

Eldo Barkhuizen

THE REPLACED APOSTLE

He Himself gave some *apostles* . . . for the
building up of the body of Christ, till
we all come to . . . a perfect man, to
the measure of the stature of
the fullness of Christ.
(Ephesians 4:11–13)

Contents

Foreword

His summation at the end of the book best describes what Mr Barkhuizen has set out to accomplish:

In this book I have attempted – from Scripture – to show that the ministry of the apostle was meant to continue into the second century and right up to the present. *Had the apostolic ministry continued, church history would have been very different from what has unfolded over the last two thousand years*, and the modern church would be a blazing city on a hill – illuminating the world – instead of the haunted ruin we largely see in the West today.

That conclusion is so unusual that its effect is rather stunning! The Roman, Eastern Orthodox and Anglican churches assert that it was their 'bishops' in 'apostolic succession' who *succeeded* to the authority of the apostles, but not that those bishops *are* apostles. Most Protestant denominational leaders find those episcopal claims very unacceptable – imagine their reaction to the idea that what God wants is not 'monarchical bishops', but actual *apostles*!

As the book's title implies, Mr Barkhuizen gives the 'devil his due' with regard to satanic influence within the history of the Christian Church. A large portion of this short but excellent work is given over to examples of how the church leaders made some bad decisions by altering a number of patterns clearly evident within the inspired writings of the New Testament.

The central example of that altered pattern was to gradually cease being a community of genuine disciples of Jesus and of His painfully specific teachings – genuine disciples who had each experientially received the same anointing of the Holy Spirit promised by Jesus. The Holy Spirit, as Mr Barkhuizen demonstrates, had raised up the ministry of Spirit-anointed 'apostles'. What the church replaced God's pattern with was a new and man-made ministry of monarchical 'bishops', kinglike leaders placed *above* the original leaders of the local church, the elders.

He demonstrates how the internal evidence of the New Testament makes it very clear that the 'bishop' (Greek: *episkopos* or 'overseer') was simply a synonym for the 'elder' (Greek: *presbyteros*), a term describing their function as the team of elders providing oversight over the local Christian community. He spends ample time analysing the influence Ignatius of Antioch had in creating this change. The process by which this evolved was complex enough that the author would have had to double the size of the book to do it justice. Perhaps a future revision will be able to accomplish that goal?

I would give *The Replaced Apostle* a solid 'A' for being *unusually* surrendered to the plain sense of the New

Testament writings and for looking at church history through an intelligently critical mind that is also carefully and solidly apostolic.

Reed K. Merino BA, MDiv

Preface

This book is the second edition of *The Missing Apostle*, which I wrote in 2021. However, I've renamed it *The Replaced Apostle*, which makes the book's theme clearer to avoid reader confusion. I've also added new material, following comments readers of the first edition made.

This book will appeal to readers who wonder why, very early in church history, the apostle's ministry disappeared. How could this happen and how did it affect the course of the church's history from that time until the present?

The Replaced Apostle is a general overview of what happened and is not meant to be an exhaustive look at the events surrounding the apostle's disappearance. To get an in-depth understanding, the reader would have to read extensively the writings of church fathers such as Irenaeus, Tertullian and Jerome, among others.

I wish to express my especial thanks to former Episcopal priest Reed K. Merino for his friendship, for his enthusiastic reception of this book and for his many valuable comments, which have helped me make this a better book.

As iron sharpens iron,
So a man sharpens the countenance of his friend.
(Proverbs 27:17)

Introduction

Go to any mid-sized town in the UK, America or Australia. Somewhere on a street you will find a building with a sign at the front that says, for example, 'First Baptist Church' or 'St Thomas's Catholic Church', or perhaps down a side road a large warehouse-type building decked out like a nightclub and supposed to be a place of Christian worship.

Step inside any of these buildings on a Sunday morning and observe what goes on during its service.

In the warehouse-type building you see rows of flashing coloured lights at the front and fake smoke wafting over the stage, a young woman in tight jeans moaning into a microphone and behind her an assortment of scruffy guitarists and a drummer banging away. After an hour of ear-splitting noise punctuated with slower, softer sounds, a long-haired young man in a Che Guevara T-shirt, ripped jeans and arms covered in tattoos, steps up to the podium and preaches a sermon on self-esteem.

Now open your New Testament and compare what you have just witnessed – or see in most buildings labelled a 'church' – with the way the early church functioned. Clearly, the two styles are light years apart.

But how did the modern church drift so far from the blueprint Jesus and His apostles laid out for us over two thousand years ago? To solve the mystery, we have to travel back into the mists of time. In fact, as far back as the second century AD, as we will see in the chapters that follow.

1
The master builder

As a wise master builder I have laid the foundation [in Corinth], and another builds on it. (1 Corinthians 3:10)

Introduction

Jesus told His disciples He would 'build' His church and the gates of Hades would 'not prevail against it' (Matthew 16:18). If we picture a building, we see a structure made, say, of blocks of shaped stones fitted together. Before a saw shapes these stones, they are rough and unattractive, *useless* in their unworked form, and are just a pile of stones.

To become part of a building each stone has to be lifted from where it lies and taken to a workroom where a stone mason can measure, saw and chip the stone into a useful shape. This process takes time, as the stone block has to fit precisely with the blocks above, below and beside it.

The first part of the building the builder has to get right is the foundation. There is no point in building a perfect wall if the foundation is shaky (see my book *Six Foundation Stones* for an in-depth look at the Christian's spiritual foundation, based on Hebrews 6:1–2). The apostle Paul describes himself as a 'wise master builder' and says he laid the 'foundation' of the church in Corinth. What is this foundation? Paul tells us it is Jesus Christ.

The heart of the gospel, the good news, Paul preached was *Christ Himself.* Paul says Christ 'died for our sins', was 'buried' and 'rose again the third day' (1 Corinthians 15:3–4). This is what Paul preached whenever he proclaimed the gospel, the 'foundation' he laid in the towns and cities he visited.

However, to be complete a building needs not only a foundation but walls to rest on that foundation and a roof to cover the walls and protect the house.

Writing to the Corinthian Christians, Paul says the church is 'God's building' (1 Corinthians 3:9), and to the Ephesians says in Christ 'the whole building, being fitted together, grows into a holy temple in the Lord, in whom [they] also are being built together for a dwelling place of God in the Spirit' (Ephesians 2: 21–22).

The building project is a process, for the 'stones', the individual Christians, must have their rough edges chipped off, so these stones can fit flush together. As each Christian becomes conformed to the image of Christ, a uniformity of Christlikeness among the 'stones' occurs, and the church becomes more and more a 'dwelling place of God in the Spirit'.

The apostle is the one who oversees this process. So, his ministry is a vital part of the continuing growth of the Christians in his care.

Who was an apostle?

Strong's Concordance says an apostle was a 'messenger', 'one commissioned by another to represent him in some way, especially a man sent out by Jesus Christ Himself to preach the Gospel'. The word 'apostle' comes from the Greek word *apostellō*, meaning 'to send' or 'send away'. J.B. Lightfoot in his commentary on Galatians says, 'The "apostle" is not only the messenger, but the delegate of the person who sends him. He is entrusted with a mission, his powers conferred upon him' (*St. Paul's Epistle to the Galatians*, p. 314). E.D. Burton says the apostle is 'a representative, one commissioned by another to represent him in some way' (*The Office of Apostle in the Early Church*, p. 562).

First, Jesus' 'disciples' spent time in His presence, learning about God's kingdom and watching Him driving out demons and healing the sick. And then, as part of their training, he appointed them as 'apostles' – 'sent ones' – to take the same message to the villages of Israel, also casting out demons and healing sick people.

For three years, before Jesus ascended to heaven, the twelve chosen disciples learned from their Master, who prepared them for their ministry of establishing and nurturing the early church.

The apostle Paul tells us the church was 'built on the foundation of the apostles and prophets', with Jesus being the 'chief corner' (Ephesians 2:20). In other words, God's church was built on the foundation of the apostles' teaching and service. Without their work, there would have been no church. Jesus built His church through His teaching, written down mainly in the Gospels, and proclaimed by the Twelve. As well as through their casting out demons and healing the sick, which ended the rule of Satan in people's lives, replacing it with the rule of God.

In Revelation, the last book of the Bible, an angel shows the apostle John the heavenly Jerusalem, a city with a wall resting on twelve foundation stones (Revelation 21:19–20), which points to the twelve apostles Jesus appointed while on earth – although Matthias replaced Judas after the latter's suicide.

What did an apostle do?

The apostles

- preached the gospel where it had not been preached before (Romans 15:20)
- started new churches (1 Corinthians 3:10)
- taught doctrine – they passed on to others what they had heard from Jesus Himself and later, after Jesus had ascended, from the Holy Spirit (John 16:12–15; Acts 2:42)

- did 'many signs and wonders' (Acts 2:43; 5:12; 9:33; 2 Corinthians 12:12)
- powerfully gave witness to Jesus' resurrection (Acts 4:33)
- distributed to the poorer Christians money brought in by the wealthier ones (Acts 4:35)
- pronounced judgement on lying Christians (Acts 5:3–10)
- through the laying on of hands ordained deacons (Acts 6:6)
- through the laying on of hands prayed for water-baptized believers to receive the Holy Spirit (Acts 8:14–18)
- raised the dead (Acts 9:40)
- appointed (ordained) elders in every city where Christians met (Acts 14:23; Titus 1:5)
- worked together with the church elders to settle doctrinal disputes (Acts 15; 16:4)
- performed signs that showed they were true apostles and that perhaps only apostles performed (2 Corinthians 12:12)
- equipped Christians for the work of ministry (Ephesians 4:12)
- built up the body of Christ (Ephesians 4:12)
- sent instructions to the churches in the form of letters, which later became Scripture (2 Peter 3:15–16)

In short, apostles were the pioneer ministers of the church. They went to places where the gospel had not been heard before, set up new churches and oversaw those churches, helping the Christians to grow to maturity and exercise ministries of their own.

The New Testament mentions three types of apostles: (1) Jesus Himself, (2) the twelve apostles Jesus chose at the beginning of His ministry and (3) apostles appointed after Jesus ascended to heaven.

Let us look at each of these in turn.

Jesus Himself

The anonymous writer of the book of Hebrews calls Jesus the 'Apostle and High Priest of our confession' (Hebrews 3:1). God the Father sent Jesus to earth to save sinners, heal the sick and cast out demons. Jesus also revealed the character of His Father and taught on the kingdom of God. Jesus was the first 'sent one' or apostle.

In John's Gospel, Jesus thirty-four times uses the expression 'sent Me' of the Father's sending Him. For example, 'I do not seek my own will but the will of the Father who *sent Me*' (John 5:30); and 'the Father who *sent Me* bears witness of Me' (John 8:18). The Father's sending Jesus is one of the main themes of John's Gospel.

The original Twelve

Early in His teaching ministry Jesus walked by the Sea of Galilee. There he saw two fishermen who were brothers, Simon (Peter) and his brother Andrew. Jesus called them to follow Him, and immediately they left their nets behind and followed Him.

Going on from there, Jesus saw two other brothers, also fishermen, James and John, in their fishing boat on the shore with their father, Zebedee, mending their nets. Jesus also called James and John, who immediately followed Him, leaving behind both their boat and father (Matthew 4:18–23).

Later in Matthew's Gospel we read that Jesus 'came to His own city'; most likely Capernaum (Matthew 9:1; see Matthew 4:13). There Jesus saw Matthew, a tax collector, sitting at his booth, and called him to follow Him. Matthew rose, left the booth and followed Jesus (Matthew 9:9).

Matthew does not tell us how Jesus called His remaining seven disciples. To find out who they were we have to turn to Mark 3:14–19: Philip, Bartholomew, Thomas, James, Thaddaeus, Simon the Zealot and Judas Iscariot (see also Luke 6:13–16).

As we saw above, these twelve men were first known as 'disciples'. But after Jesus gave them authority over demons and the ability to heal sicknesses, they became 'apostles' (Matthew 10:1–2). And after He gave them this authority, Jesus 'sent' them out to preach the good news of God's kingdom, to heal the sick and cast out demons (Matthew 10:5–8).

The apostle Paul

Travelling on the hot, dusty road to Damascus, in Syria, was a young Jewish Pharisee, Saul, who hated Jesus and His followers.

Saul had witnessed and approved of the murder of the first Christian martyr, Stephen, and had then gone on to make 'havoc' of the church, entering the houses of the Christians in Israel and dragging men and women off to prison (Acts 7:58; 8:3).

Not satisfied with imprisoning Christians only in Israel, having received letters from the high priest to the synagogues of Damascus, Saul decided to journey to the Syrian city. There he would search for Christians who attended the synagogues, seize them and then bring them back captive to Jerusalem (Acts 9:1–2). But Saul was about to have a shocking encounter that would dramatically change the course of his life.

As he drew near the city, suddenly a bright light blazed around him and he fell to the ground. Next, he heard a voice saying, 'Saul, Saul, why are you persecuting Me?' Saul asked who was speaking to him, and heard the voice say, 'I am Jesus, whom you are persecuting' (Acts 9:3–5).

Luke, the writer of the book of Acts, says Saul, struck blind by the light, 'trembling and astonished', asked Jesus what he should do. Jesus told him to enter Damascus, where he would be given instructions. Led by the hand, the young man entered the city and stayed at the house of a certain Judas, where Saul, still blind, neither ate nor drank for three days (Acts 9:6–9).

Jesus spoke in a vision to Ananias, a Christian living in Damascus. He told Ananias to go to the house Saul was staying in and pray for him. Ananias was fearful, for he had heard of Saul and how he had persecuted the church in Israel and that he had come to Damascus to persecute the Christians there too. But the Lord told Ananias, Saul 'is a chosen vessel of Mine to bear My name before Gentiles, kings, and the children of Israel' (Acts 9:10–15).

Years later, after an adventurous – and dangerous – life of service to Jesus, the aged Saul (now known by the Greek name Paul), writing to Timothy, calls himself 'an apostle of Jesus Christ' (1 Timothy 1:1; see also 2 Timothy 1:1). Paul had most likely seen the risen Jesus after his Damascus road experience when he was 'caught up to the third heaven' and no doubt received insight there on his future ministry as an apostle and on the blueprint for how God's church should function (2 Corinthians 12:2–6).

Writing to the church in the Greek city of Corinth, Paul describes the church not only as a building, but as a *field* of plants (1 Corinthians 3:9). For a field to yield a harvest of ripe, healthy wheat, at least three things have to happen:

1 The field has to be planted with healthy seed.
2 The seed has to be watered regularly.
3 The growing crop must be kept free of pests and diseases that will harm it.

Paul says one plants and another waters. He says he planted the seed, and the Christian teacher Apollos watered it (1 Corinthians 3:6).

If we liken the field to the kingdom of God, the 'seeds' planted in that field are the 'wheat' Jesus describes in His parable of the wheat and tares (Matthew 13:24–30).

The pests and diseases that spoil a crop can be likened to false teachers and their poisonous doctrines. The churches Paul established in Galatia fell prey to such wolves in sheep's clothing, as did the church in Corinth (Galatians 1:6–9; 2 Corinthians 11:3–4).

Paul would go to a city and begin proclaiming the good news (gospel) of Jesus' death on the cross for humanity's sins and His burial and resurrection from the dead. Some of the apostle's hearers would respond by deciding to become followers (disciples) of the risen Jesus, repenting from their sins, being baptized in water and then being prayed for to receive the Holy Spirit (see for example Acts 8:14–18). These new disciples, formerly children of the devil and thus bad seed, worthless to God or man, were now transformed into useful 'wheat' seeds.

By his preaching the death and resurrection of Jesus, baptizing new believers in water and then praying for them to receive the Holy Spirit, Paul 'planted' good seed in God's field.

But for that seed to grow and ripen into a wheat plant, which could be harvested at the end of the growing season and be stored in a barn, the seed needed watering. Which is where God-appointed teachers such as Apollos did what they were called to do. This is what Paul means when he describes apostles, prophets, evangelists and shepherd-teachers in the church as 'speaking the truth in love', which builds up and matures the Christian hearers in their faith (Ephesians 4:11–15).

As we saw above, Paul also describes God's church as a *building*. The apostle compares his ministry to that of a 'wise master builder'. The Greek word the NKJV translates as 'master builder' is *architektōn*, which is a 'master-craftsman' or 'architect'. HELPS Word-studies says this term means 'someone responsible from the beginning to the end of success . . . of a building'.

The apostle's is thus the most important ministry in God's church, as the apostle *lays the foundation* of a new assembly of Christians (church) and then *oversees the maturing* of that assembly into a holy, perfected group of believers. Paul writes to the church in Ephesus (in modern-day Turkey):

> the household of God, having been built on the *foundation of the apostles and prophets*, Jesus Christ Himself being the chief cornerstone, in whom the whole building, being fitted together, grows into a holy temple in the Lord, in whom you also are being *built together* for a dwelling place of God in the Spirit. (Ephesians 2:19–22)

The 'foundation' the apostle lays is accurate, anointed teaching about who Jesus is and why He came to earth. Without the perfect life, death and resurrection of Jesus, there would be no church. He is both the 'cornerstone' of the church's foundation – that which holds the foundation together – and the foundation itself. Paul writes, 'For no other foundation can anyone lay than that which is laid, which is Jesus Christ' (1 Corinthians 3:11).

The heart of Paul's message was Jesus Himself. The core of the good news, 'gospel', Paul and the apostles preached was 'Christ died for our sins', 'He was buried' and 'He rose again the third day' (1 Corinthians 15:3–4).

2

Just the Twelve and Paul?

Nor did we seek glory from men, either from you or from others, when we might have made demands as apostles of Christ. (1 Thessalonians 2:6)

In the previous chapter we looked at the first twelve apostles and the apostle Paul. Here I will point out another seven men in the New Testament who are described as, or implied to be, apostles. But first, let me clear up some widespread false teaching.

What qualifies a man for apostleship?

In his online article 'Are There Still Apostles Today?' Nathan Busenitz says the first qualification of an apostle is that he 'had to be an eyewitness of the resurrected Christ (Acts 1:22; 10:39–41; 1 Cor. 9:1; 15:7–8'. We will examine each of these texts in turn.

Acts 1:22 relates to the choice of Matthias to replace Judas the betrayer, who had hanged himself. To qualify as one of the Twelve, yes, Matthias had to be a witness of Jesus' resurrection.

Acts 10:39–41 records the words of the apostle Peter, who says the Eleven were 'witnesses' of Jesus' ministry, death and resurrection.

1 Corinthians 9:1 has the words of the apostle Paul, who says, 'Am I not an apostle? . . . Have I not seen Jesus Christ our Lord?'

1 Corinthians 15:7–8 again has Paul saying he saw the resurrected Christ.

What Dr Busenitz seems to miss is that whereas being a witness of the resurrected Christ was a requirement for a man to be one of the Twelve, as seen in the above verses, this was not the case with Paul. Paul does not say that seeing Christ qualified him for apostleship, but merely that he saw Christ. To say that Paul's seeing Christ was one of the *requirements* for his being an apostle is going beyond the plain meaning of the text.

This argument that the Twelve (and Paul) were the last apostles in history, based on the texts above, is incorrect – which I will prove in the rest of this chapter.

The four qualifications for apostleship laid out in the New Testament are as follows:

1 *Calling*: Jesus called certain men to fulfil the office of apostle (Matthew 10:1; Romans 1:1).
2 *Holiness*: apostles were holy men (Ephesians 3:5).
3 *Faithfulness*: apostles were faithful men (Matthew 24:45).

4 *Wisdom*: apostles were wise men (Matthew 24:45).

If, as many today claim, having seen the risen Jesus was one of the requirements for being an apostle, then Paul would have been the final apostle in church history. But, according to the New Testament, was Paul indeed the last of the apostles?

Were there apostles other than the Twelve and Paul?

Yes, we read of other men who were apostles in addition to the Twelve and Paul.

Barnabas

The first time we hear of Barnabas is in Acts 4:36, where Luke tells us Barnabas was a Jew from the tribe of Levi and a Cypriot. His name was Joses, but the apostles in Jerusalem nicknamed him 'Barnabas', which means 'Son of Encouragement' – Barnabas was an encourager!

He appears again in Acts 9 after the conversion of Saul (Paul). When Saul came to Jerusalem, he wanted to join the Christians there, but they were afraid of him because of the way he had hunted them down before his conversion. Barnabas, however, stepped in and introduced Saul to the apostles, to whom Saul described his conversion and preaching about Jesus in Damascus. The 'Son of Encouragement' played a huge part in Saul's life.

After the martyrdom of Stephen, which Saul approved of, some Christians travelled north-west to Cyprus and northwards to Phoenicia and Antioch. In Antioch they preached to Greek-speaking Jews known as Hellenists, and many of these Jews, believing on Jesus, were converted (Acts 11:19–27). This was the start of a new church that was to become one of the leading centres of Christianity in the ancient world.

When the Jerusalem church heard of the move of God's Spirit in Antioch, they sent Barnabas there. Having arrived, he encouraged them to continue with Jesus and, Luke says, 'a great many people were added to the Lord' (Acts 11:24).

In the meantime, Saul had returned to his home city of Tarsus, located about 100 miles (160 km) north-west of Antioch.

Barnabas went to Tarsus to find Saul and brought him to the church in Antioch, where the two men taught the assembled believers for a year (Acts 11:25–26). This was the start of a partnership between Barnabas and Saul that would lead to some thrilling adventures, described in the book of Acts.

Sometime later, while fasting and praying with other leaders in the church at Antioch, the Holy Spirit said, 'Now separate to me Barnabas and Saul for the work to which I have called them' (Acts 13:2). These leaders, having fasted and prayed, laid hands on Barnabas and Saul and sent them away. This began a preaching tour to various parts of Asia Minor.

In the city of Lystra Luke describes the two men as 'the apostles Barnabas and Saul' (Acts 14:14) – we see here that Barnabas is called an apostle.

Silas

The first we hear of Silas is when the church at Antioch sent him and another man to Jerusalem along with (the renamed) Paul and Barnabas (Acts 15:22).

Sometime later Paul said to Barnabas that they should revisit the Christians in the cities they had journeyed through on their first preaching tour. Barnabas wanted to take his relative Mark with them, but Mark had deserted them on their earlier preaching tour and Paul was determined not to take Mark. The disagreement between the two apostles became so sharp that they parted, and Paul chose Silas to go with him (Acts 15:36–40).

When they reached the city of Lystra, Paul chose a young man named Timothy, highly respected among the local churches, to join them as they continued on their journey strengthening the churches in various cities (Acts 16:1–3).

Thessalonica was one of the cities Paul, Silas and Timothy visited (Acts 17:1–4). When we turn to the first chapter of both the letter of 1 Thessalonians and 2 Thessalonians, we see that the greeting in verse 1 is from 'Paul, Silvanus, and Timothy'. So, the authors of both letters are the three men mentioned.

The *Holman Bible Dictionary* says 'Silas' seems to be the Greek form of the Latin name 'Silvanus'. Thus, Silas and Silvanus were the same person.

In 1 Thessalonians 2:6 the three men describe themselves as 'apostles of Christ' – so, Silas/Silvanus and Timothy, in addition to Paul, were apostles. *Note*: the author of every letter in the New Testament – including the co-authored 1 and 2 Thessalonians – was an apostle.

Timothy

As we saw above, 1 Thessalonians clearly calls Timothy an apostle. The two letters Paul wrote to Timothy, 1 and 2 Timothy, near the end of Paul's life, are detailed instructions for how the young apostle should conduct himself in God's church and how that church should be structured and function. These are the blueprint Paul wanted Timothy to use and share with others God would raise up for leadership in His church, and *this blueprint was meant to guide the church until the return of Jesus* (1 Timothy 3:15; 2 Timothy 2:2).

Epaphroditus

The New Testament mentions Epaphroditus just twice. He was a member of the church in Philippi (Philippians 2:25; 4:18). In his letter to the Philippians Paul calls him 'my brother, fellow worker, and fellow soldier' and then adds that Epaphroditus is the Philippian church's 'apostle' (2:25). The NKJV translates 'apostle' here as 'messenger', which is a possible translation. So, was Epaphroditus merely a 'messenger' or was he an 'apostle' of the Philippian church?

As Paul calls him his 'fellow worker' and 'fellow soldier', perhaps 'apostle' is more appropriate. Timothy, another apostle, is also called Paul's 'fellow worker' (1 Thessalonians 3:2). The word 'fellow soldier' appears in just one other place in the New Testament, where Paul describes Archippus in this way (Philemon 1:2). *Thayer's Greek Lexicon* says a 'fellow soldier' is 'an associate in labors and conflicts for the cause of Christ'.

Tychicus

Tychicus appears five times in the pages of the New Testament. We read in Acts 20:4 that he was one of Paul's companions. Paul sent him as his representative to Ephesus and Colossae, probably carrying the letters of Ephesians and Colossians (Ephesians 6:21; Colossians 4:7; 2 Timothy 4:12). As a 'sent one' (Greek, *apostellō*) and part of Paul's ministry team, it is possible that Tychicus was also an 'apostle' (*apostolos*).

Andronicus

Mentioned just once in the New Testament, Andronicus appears in the list of people in Rome Paul greets at the end of his letter to the Romans (Romans 16:7). Paul says Andronicus is one of his 'countrymen' (he was Jewish), a 'fellow prisoner' 'of note among the apostles' who was a Christian before Paul. There is an ambiguity here, however, as Paul may be saying Andronicus was highly respected by the apostles rather than that he was an apostle himself.

Junias

Alongside Andronicus Paul greets Junias, who was also Jewish, a prisoner and outstanding among the apostles (see the above comment). As to whether Junias was a woman rather than a man, and thus perhaps a female apostle, see the next chapter, where I examine this thorny issue.

False apostles

When writing to the church in Corinth, Paul mentions 'false apostles' visiting the church (2 Corinthians 11:13). Similarly, in the book of Revelation Jesus speaks of 'those who say they are apostles and are not' (Revelation 2:2). The fact that men were visiting various churches and presenting themselves as apostles shows that these churches accepted that the original Twelve and Paul were *not the only apostles in existence*. If apostleship were exclusive to Paul and the Twelve, then it would be pointless for men to go from church to church calling themselves apostles – these churches would have rejected such 'apostles' outright!

3
A female apostle?

Of these *men* who have accompanied us . . . one of these must become a witness with us of His resurrection. (Acts 1:21–22; my emphasis)

What Paul says about women leading in God's church

Writing to Timothy, Paul says:

Let a woman learn in silence with all submission. And *I do not permit a woman to teach or to have authority over a man*, but to be in silence. For Adam was formed first, then Eve. And Adam was not deceived, but the woman *being deceived,* fell into transgression. (1 Timothy 2:11–14; my emphases)

The older apostle, here giving instructions to the younger apostle, says women in the church (1) must learn in silence and have a submissive attitude, (2) are not allowed to teach and (3) cannot have authority over a man, again mentioning that they must stay silent. Paul gives two reasons for these instructions: (1) in God's created order Adam was created before Eve, implying that Adam was her head (compare 1 Corinthians 11:3, 8–9), and (2) whereas Eve was deceived, the man was not – with the implication that Satan can deceive women easier than he can deceive men.

Addressing the church in Corinth, which had chaotic meetings when its members assembled, Paul says:

> Let your women keep silent in the churches, for they are not permitted to speak; but they are to be submissive, as the law also says. And if they want to learn something, let them ask their own husbands at home; for *it is shameful for women to speak in church.* (1 Corinthians 14:34–35)

Again, the mention of women being 'silent' and 'submissive' when assembling with the men of the church. Women wanting an explanation of something they heard during a meeting were not to call out, but to ask their husbands at home (who presumably would be able to supply an answer to the wife's question).

To modern ears Paul's instructions seem outrageous. However, God had shown Paul the divine blueprint of how His church should be structured and function, and Paul was simply repeating this to the Corinthian church and in his letters to Timothy. *This blueprint – despite shifts in cultural world views over many centuries – was meant to continue until the return of Jesus to set up His thousand-year kingdom on earth.*

Apostles are the most important leaders in God's church, and Scripture unbendingly excludes women from holding this office. Interestingly, none of the Twelve was a woman, and when the apostles chose a replacement for the traitor Judas, only *men* were put forward as candidates.

Priscilla

Priscilla, the wife of a Jew by the name of Aquila, lived with her husband in Corinth. They were tentmakers and Paul, because he had the same trade, stayed in their house when he came to Corinth (Acts 18:1–3).

After staying in Corinth 'many days', Paul set sail for Ephesus, taking Aquila and Priscilla with him. Leaving them in Ephesus, Paul sailed on to Jerusalem (Acts 18:18–19). In Ephesus Aquila and Priscilla used their house as a meeting place for Ephesian Christians – they had a 'church' in their house (1 Corinthians 16:19).

Eventually the husband-and-wife team returned to Italy, where they had lived before relocating to Corinth. In the list of people he greets at the end of his letter to the Christians at Rome, Paul says, 'Greet Priscilla and Aquila, my fellow workers in Christ' (Romans 16:3).

Aquila and Priscilla were Paul's 'fellow workers' and helped him in his ministry, perhaps by housing him when he needed accommodation and by giving him extra money for his support. The apostle had a travelling ministry, but this couple stayed in two locations (first Corinth and then Ephesus) for some time, before going back to Italy (Rome). Nowhere is there any hint that either was an apostle, with oversight over a number of churches. Also, as we saw above, Paul would not have sanctioned a woman leading in the church, although this is common today in many groups that claim to be Christian churches.

In the New Testament, local church leaders, known as 'elders', 'pastors (shepherds)' or 'overseers/bishops' (three terms for the same office), are *always male* and *always plural*. There is no example in the New Testament of a 'pastor', 'senior pastor', or 'lead elder' assisted by an 'assistant pastor', 'junior pastor', 'worship pastor', 'youth pastor' – *or any other kind of 'pastor', singular* – running a church. Local churches were overseen by co-equal male 'elders' who served the flock and did not lord it over them by using the title 'Pastor' so and so.

Today many churches have a husband and wife 'leadership team', a male/female 'minister'/'pastor', assisted by 'elders' (also sometimes wrongly called 'deacons') in steering their ship, or all kinds of other offices mentioned nowhere in the New Testament – such as 'archdeacon', 'vicar', 'curate', 'associate vicar', 'lay minister', 'major', 'secretary', 'treasurer', 'property steward', 'church-warden', 'health and safety officer', and so on. Such denominations have deformed God's simple blueprint for His church – *set in stone in Scripture.*

There is no mention that Priscilla or her husband, Aquila, were elders or ordained in any way, although it is possible Aquila was an elder, as he and Priscilla hosted a local church in their house in Ephesus and later in Rome (1 Corinthians 16:19; Romans 16:3–5).

Lydia

After Paul, Silas and Timothy had journeyed to the city of Troas (Troy) and met up with Luke, the physician and author of Acts, Paul had a vision in the night. He saw a Macedonian man who begged him to go to Macedonia to help the man and his people (Acts 16:8–9).

Sensing the urgency of the vision, Paul and his companions set sail from Troas shortly afterwards and came to Philippi, the main city of that area of Macedonia, in around AD 49 (Acts 16:10–12).

On the Sabbath day the four men went to the riverside, where they found women who had met there to pray. Among these was Lydia, a businesswoman from the city of Thyatira in Asia Minor (modern Turkey) who sold expensive purple cloth. Luke says, as a result of Paul's conversation with the women about Jesus, Lydia believed in Him and, after she and her household had been baptized, begged the four men to stay in her house (Acts 16:14–15).

Later, after Paul and Silas were unjustly thrown into jail in Philippi, the Philippian jailer and his household also believed in Jesus and were baptized in water (Acts 16:29–34). Now there were two believing households in Philippi, and perhaps the start of two house churches.

The Greek word used for Lydia's and the Philippian jailer's 'household' is *oikos*, which means a house or the people living in that house (Acts 16:15, 31). We do not know whether Lydia had any family members living with her, but she likely owned slaves, as was common in those days. We also do not know how many people lived in Lydia's house. The same applies to the Philippian jailer, although he might not have owned any slaves. Luke does not tell us.

However, the members of Lydia's and the jailer's households formed the core of the first assembly of Christians in Philippi.

By the time Paul wrote his letter to the Philippian church from Rome around AD 61, where he was under house arrest (Acts 28:16, 20, 30), about twelve years after he had left Philippi, there were 'overseers/bishops' (elders) and deacons in Philippi. *Note*: Paul does not address his letter to the 'pastor' or 'senior pastor' of the church at Philippi!

Although Lydia's name appears twice in Acts 16, and she might have hosted the first Philippian church in her house, there is no hint that she was an elder or apostle, and her name does not appear again in the New Testament.

A side point regarding Lydia's and the jailer's households is that those who promote infant baptism claim there 'must' have been infants in at least one of these households, which means the Bible teaches infant baptism. In my book *Six Foundation Stones* I have an in-depth discussion on this argument from silence.

Phoebe

Writing to the church in Rome, Paul commends a woman by the name of Phoebe (Romans 16:1–2). In two verses we learn that she is a 'sister' of the Christians, a 'servant' of the church in Cenchrea, that she had business to attend to in Rome and that she has been a 'supporter' of many Christians, including Paul himself.

Paul speaks respectfully and tenderly when he refers to Phoebe as 'our sister', one of the members of God's family. It seems likely she was the courier who took Paul's letter to the church at Rome. The apostle must have had great confidence in her to entrust her with one of his most important letters.

The word used for 'servant' in verse 1 is *diakonos*. Some have said Phoebe was a deacon or deaconess of the Cenchrean church, but this is impossible.

In his first letter to the apostle Timothy, where Paul gives the younger man instructions on how God's church should operate, he deals with the qualifications for deaconship. He says the deacons' 'wives' must be reverent and that deacons 'must be the husbands of one wife' and rule their children and houses well (1 Timothy 3:12–13). Clearly, deacons must be male.

We see this also in Acts in the apostles' instructions for the choice of seven deacons, who are to be '*men . . .* full of the Holy Spirit and wisdom' (Acts 6:3, 5–6). Although these seven are not called 'deacons', they fulfil the function of deacons. So, it seems clear this was their office. *Note*: the word used in Acts 6:3 for 'men' comes from the Greek word *anēr*, which means 'a male human being' or 'a husband' (*Strong's Concordance*).

Paul's instructions to Timothy about deacons exclude women from holding this office. However, despite Paul's teaching, 'deaconesses' appeared in church history from the second century AD onwards.

Like Lydia, Phoebe seems to have been a business-woman, which would have provided her with the funds to be a 'supporter' or helper of many Christians, including Paul. The Greek word for 'supporter' or 'helper' used to describe this respected woman is *prostatis*. It means a female guardian or patroness, 'caring for the affairs of others and aiding them with their resources' (*Thayer's Greek Lexicon*).

Again, the text says nowhere that Phoebe, although an honoured member of the church, was an ordained minister. She was neither a 'deaconess' nor an apostle!

Euodia and Syntyche

These were two women in the church at Philippi who had a disagreement between them. We do not know what this was, but Paul begs them to 'be of the same mind in the Lord'. He also says they strove with him in the gospel and describes them as his 'fellow workers' (Philippians 4:2–3).

The Greek word for 'strive together', *synathleō*, Paul uses here appears just twice in the New Testament, with both occurrences in Philippians. He uses it first in Philippians 1:27 when he urges the Philippian Christians to be of 'one soul', 'striving together' for 'the faith of the gospel'. *Strong's Concordance* says *synathleō* means 'I compete together with others, cooperate vigorously with'.

The Greek word Paul uses for 'fellow labourer' is *synergos*, which means 'a companion in work, fellow-worker' (*Thayer's Greek Lexicon*). Paul uses the same word for his relationship with Priscilla and Aquila (Romans 16:3), Urbanus (Romans 16:9), Timothy (Romans 16:21), Titus (2 Corinthians 8:23), Epaphroditus (Philippians 2:25), Philemon (Philemon 1:1), Demas and Luke (Philemon 1:24).

Euodia and Syntyche were Paul's 'fellow workers' and strove together with him in the gospel, but did they hold an office in the church? Had they been ordained as elders, deaconesses or apostles?

In their article 'Euodia, Syntyche and the Role of Syzygos: Phil 4:2–3', R.G. Fellows and A.C. Stewart describe the two women as 'church leaders' and 'congregational leaders'. And H. Lockyer in his *All the Women of the Bible* goes so far as to call Euodia and Syntyche 'deaconesses'. However, the text of Philippians 4:2–3 says nothing about these women being 'leaders' or 'deaconesses' of the Philippian church, but only that they were Paul's 'fellow workers' and strove together with him in the gospel.

What exactly Paul means by this is not further explained, and as we saw earlier in this chapter the apostle is crystal clear that women are not allowed to lead or teach doctrine in God's church. *Note*: there is *no example in the New Testament of an ordained woman in any church*. Furthermore, nowhere do we read in the New Testament that this blueprint should change to conform with the views of the satanic society in which the church lives. When the world view of the surrounding society invades and takes over the church, the latter ceases to be God's church, but instead becomes a 'synagogue [assembly] of Satan' (Revelation 2:9; 3:9).

'Junia'

Included in the list of Christians Paul greets in his letter to the Romans is Junia(s) (Romans 16:7). Some have translated this as 'Junia' (feminine) and others as 'Junias' (masculine). Out of 60 English Bible versions I compared, 16 (around 27%) translate the name as 'Junias'. So, over two-thirds of these Bible translators believed the *feminine* version of the name, Junia, is correct.

The Greek form of the word, as it appears in the New Testament, is Iounian, which is in the accusative (objective) case. The nominative (subjective) case is *either* Iounia (Junia) or Iounias (Junias). *Strong's Concordance* and the *New American Standard Exhaustive Concordance* state that Romans 16:7 refers to Iounias, the masculine form.

The balanced, scholarly cbmw.org article 'A Female Apostle?' makes the following points in favour of 'Junias':

1 The masculine names in Romans 16:14–15, Patrobas, Hermas and Olympas follow the same Greek format as Junias.

2 During New Testament times Latin names were some-times shortened to Greek ones. For example, Silvanus was shortened to Silas (Acts 17:10; 1 Thessalonians 1:1). So Junias could be a shortened form of one of the common Latin names Junianus, Junianius or Junilius.

3 When a slave was freed after serving well, that slave took the master's family name, but not as the name appeared. The ending of the name was changed to '–*as*'. 'Thus, any slave freed by a master having the family name Junius would adopt the name Junias. Junius was a common family name in the Roman world.'

4 Although some scholars claim, or claim with hesitancy, that for more than the first thousand years all the church 'fathers' read the name in Romans 16:7 as 'Junia', this claim is incorrect. Epiphanius (315–403), Bishop of Salamis in Cyprus, in his *Index of Disciples* writes, 'Junias, of whom Paul makes mention, became Bishop of Apameia of Syria.'

E.D. Burton also regards Junias as a male apostle (*The Office of Apostle in the Early Church*, pp. 573–574).

4

The apostolic blueprint for God's church

Now the Spirit explicitly says that in latter times some will depart from the faith, giving heed to deceiving spirits and doctrines of demons. (1 Timothy 4:1)

Many scholars today seem to think the Twelve and Paul were the last New Testament apostles. As we saw earlier, these scholars do not regard Barnabas, Silas and Timothy, for example, as apostles – *even though Scripture gives them this title*.

Before we investigate in the next chapter the question of whether there were apostles after the close of the New Testament era, around the end of the first century AD, let us take a brief look at the structure of the apostolic church. God gave us the blueprint in the New Testament for how His church should function, *a blueprint the church was meant to follow until the return of Jesus to set up His earthly kingdom*.

The holy assembly

The word usually translated as 'church' in English Bible versions comes from the Greek word *ekklēsia*, meaning 'an assembly' or 'congregation' of people. (The English word 'ecclesiastical' comes from *ekklēsia*.) God's 'church' is not a dead building of bricks and mortar, or a cathedral of stone, but a dynamic temple of Spirit-baptized 'living stones' where He dwells by His Spirit (Ephesians 2:22; 1 Peter 2:5).

Paul says God's *ekklēsia* grows into a 'holy temple in the Lord' as the individual stones are 'fitted together' (Ephesians 2:21). Further on in his letter Paul describes the final result of this process: believers (1) united in their understanding of the Christian faith, (2) united in their knowledge of Christ, (3) being fully mature, so 'a perfect man', and (4) being completely full of Christ and thus being like Him.

But how does the *ekklēsia* reach this state of perfection? Before we look at this, have you ever heard the following teaching? 'When we believe in Jesus, all our sins – past, present and future – are taken away. We are in Christ and when the Father looks at us, He sees us clothed in Christ's righteousness. *We will be sinners until the day we die.* But that's all right, because we are clothed in Christ's righteousness, and will still go to heaven.' Although widely believed among lukewarm, compromising Christians, this is a dangerous, demonic teaching, and is not what the New Testament says. I go into this in far greater detail in my book *Six Foundation Stones,* so will not deal with it much here.

Suffice it to say, when writing to the *ekklēsia* in Rome, Paul exclaims with horror, 'How shall we who died to sin live any longer in it?' (Romans 6:2). Further on in the same letter he writes that God 'condemned sin in the flesh, that the righteous requirement of the law *might be fulfilled by us* who do not walk according to the flesh but *according to the Spirit*' (8:3–4; my emphases).

The 'living stones' who make up God's assembly are meant to live holy lives. Only those who 'live according to the Spirit', overcome, finish the race successfully and are *approved* will be allowed to enter the eternal heavenly city (Romans 8:5; 1 Corinthians 9:24; James 1:12; Revelation 2:7). Unfortunately, and deceptively, those who follow Calvinism call this 'works salvation'. However, according to the clear teaching of Scripture, *no personal holiness of character and life, no heaven* (2 Corinthians 7:1; Hebrews 12:14). See also what happened to the man who came to the wedding without a wedding garment (Matthew 22:11–13; compare Revelation 19:7–8).

The further question arises: How do the 'living stones' of God's *ekklēsia* reach this state of perfection? Paul answers this in his letter to the church in Ephesus. He says, the ascended Christ 'gave [to His *ekklēsia*] some apostles, some prophets, some evangelists, and some pastors [shepherds] and teachers', and the reason He did this was for the strengthening and maturing of the body of Christ (Ephesians 4:12). And 'speaking the truth in love' to one another in the *ekklēsia* results in those who hear such words growing up to perfection in Christ (verse 15). But before the believers can speak the truth to one another they have to *know* what that truth is! The 'living stones' learn from the apostles, prophets and teachers, after hearing an evangelist preach the gospel, or after encountering the gospel in some other way.

Apostles

As mentioned in chapter 1, Jesus chose twelve men to disciple over a period of about three years. These 'disciples' lived with Him day and night, saw the quality of His perfect life, heard His teaching and observed Him delivering people from demons and performing many miracles of healing. Jesus then sent them out to teach what they had heard from Him and to do the same miracles: 'And as you go, preach, saying, "The kingdom of heaven is at hand." Heal the sick, cleanse the lepers, raise the dead, cast out demons' (Matthew 10:7–8). Once sent out, these disciples became 'apostles', 'sent ones'.

After Jesus ascended to heaven, He continued His ministry through the men He had called and trained so carefully; although, as we know, Judas betrayed Jesus and fell away.

The apostle's ministry is the most important of the four ministries Paul mentions in Ephesians 4 (I take that of the shepherd-teacher to be one ministry, for the reason outlined below). As we saw in chapter 1, the apostle is the 'architect', the master-craftsman, of a local or group of churches in a region.

Taking Peter and Paul as examples of this 'master-craftsmanship', let us explore how they carried out their calling to be apostles. In the book he wrote, Acts, Luke the medical doctor focuses on two giants of the early church: Peter, in the first half of the book, and Paul, in the second half.

Peter

In the early part of Acts Peter spends most of his time in Jerusalem. On the day of Pentecost he preaches from the book of Joel to the astonished Jews in Jerusalem, explaining to them what has just happened. Around three thousand *repent* at Peter's preaching, are *baptized in water* and are then *baptized in the Holy Spirit* – all three steps were necessary for these people to be 'added' to the church (see Acts 8:38, 41). Spirit-baptism is a requirement to be an adopted member of God's household (Romans 8:15–17). Again, I cover this vital – and *rarely taught* – issue in far more detail in my *Six Foundation Stones* book, available from Amazon.

As mentioned earlier, accurate doctrinal teaching and the performing of miracles are two of the hallmarks of the true apostle's ministry.

At 3 p.m. one day Peter and John are on their way to the temple to pray. When they reach the gate of the temple, a lame man sitting or lying there asks them for money. Fixing his eyes on the man, Peter commands him in the name of Jesus to walk, takes him by the hand and lifts him up. The man's lameness heals and, being made completely well, he enters the temple with Peter and John, 'walking, leaping, and praising God' (Acts 3:8).

Acts records other miracles done through Peter, such as the raising of Dorcas from the dead and Peter's teaching of Cornelius the Roman centurion and his household (9:36–41; 10:34–44). Peter wrote two letters to Christians, 1 and 2 Peter, in which he lays out his thoughts on various issues. These letters became part of the New Testament canon (standard) of Scripture.

Paul

Preaching the good news of the kingdom of God, the occurrence of the miraculous, and accurate, in-depth teaching also characterized Paul's ministry.

Being sent out from the church at Antioch by the Holy Spirit, Saul (later renamed Paul) and Barnabas arrive in Cyprus. As is Paul's custom, the two men preach God's word in the synagogues they find there. Then, journeying through the island, they reach the south-western coastal city of Paphos, where an extraordinary event occurs (Acts 13:3–5).

In Paphos they find a Jew by the name of Bar-Jesus, a sorcerer and false prophet who is close to the Roman proconsul (governor) Sergius Paulus. The proconsul calls for the two apostles and wants to hear God's word, but the sorcerer opposes God's messengers and tries to influence the proconsul against them. Filled with the Holy Spirit, Paul says the sorcerer will be struck blind for a time.

At once a 'dark mist' comes upon the opposer and he is unable to see. When Sergius Paulus sees this happening, he believes in Jesus, 'being astonished at the teaching of the Lord' (Acts 13:12).

And an example of Paul's teaching ministry is when, sometime later, on another apostolic journey, he arrives in Ephesus. For three months he reasons and persuades in the synagogue, using the Old Testament Scriptures, and speaks of God's kingdom. But, meeting resistance from some of the members of the synagogue, he departs and takes with him those who believed his message. For the next two years he 'reasons' in the school of Tyrannus in Ephesus, again no doubt from the Old Testament Scriptures.

Prophets

Whereas apostles are the most important ministry in the church, the prophet comes second in importance (1 Corinthians 12:28).

HELPS Word-studies says a prophet is someone who '*speaks forth* by the inspiration of God'. The prophet proclaims God's message and sometimes foretells the future. The prophet is 'an interpreter or forth-teller of the divine will' (*Strong's Concordance*).

In his instructions to the church in Corinth Paul says the one who prophesies speaks '*edification* and *encouragement* and *comfort* to men' (1 Corinthians 14:3; my translation). The word 'edification' here means 'building up'. Quoting *Winer's Grammar*, *Thayer's Greek Lexicon*, says 'edification' means 'the act of one who promotes another's growth in Christian wisdom, piety, holiness, happiness'. The word 'encouragement' in the Greek is *paraklēsis*, and it means a 'calling to one's aid'. The word 'comfort' in 1 Corinthians 14:3, *paramythia*, appears only here in the New Testament. HELPS Word-studies says this word means 'a *speaking closely* to anyone' and expresses 'a *greater degree of tenderness*' than *paraklēsis*.

Two New Testament figures who stand out as prophets are Barnabas and Agabus.

Barnabas

We first meet Barnabas in Acts 4:36. We learn that his real name is Joses but that the apostles nicknamed him 'Barnabas', which means 'Son of Encouragement'. The Greek word for 'encouragement' in Barnabas's nickname is *paraklēsis*, mentioned above. Barnabas was such an encourager that he came to be known by this title – he stood with others, spoke up for them and encouraged them.

When Saul, the former persecutor of Christians, came to Jerusalem, he tried to associate with the Christians there. But they were too afraid to meet him. It was Barnabas who took Saul to the apostles and spoke up for him (Acts 9:26–27).

After Stephen was martyred, persecution arose against the Christians in Israel and some of these journeyed to the city of Antioch, beside the Orontes River in Syria. Situated on important trade routes, the city was also an intellectual centre of the Roman Empire, rivalling Alexandria in Egypt. It would become a major hub of Christianity in later years (Acts 11:19).

The Christians who went to Antioch carried the good news about Jesus with them and spoke to Hellenists – Jews following the Greek culture – in the city. Many of these Hellenists believed and became Christians (Acts 11:20–21).

When the church in Jerusalem heard about the conversions in Antioch, they sent Barnabas, 'a good man, full of the Holy Spirit and of faith', to the new converts. When he arrived in Antioch, he rejoiced to see the move of God there and 'encouraged' them to continue with Jesus. The word 'encouraged' here is the verb form of the noun *paraklēsis* (Acts 11:22–24).

Furthermore, not wanting to be the centre of attention, and being more concerned for the spiritual growth of the new Christians than for his own advancement, Barnabas journeyed to the nearby city of Tarsus in the west to find Saul and bring him to Antioch. Barnabas no doubt knew what a superb teacher Saul was and wanted the Christians in Antioch to benefit from Saul's deep knowledge of the Old Testament Scriptures and the revelations he had received since the heavenly light had blinded him on the Damascus road. The two men remained in Antioch and taught the Christians there for a year (Acts 11:25–26).

Luke records that in the church in Antioch were 'certain prophets and teachers' (Acts 13:1). Saul was one of these 'teachers' and Barnabas was one of the 'prophets'. While these five prophets and teachers 'ministered' to the Lord and fasted, the Holy Spirit said (presumably through a word of prophecy) He had called Barnabas and Saul to a specific work. In response, the other men laid hands on the pair and sent them away on their first apostolic journey together.

Agabus

While Barnabas and Saul were teaching the church in Antioch, a group of prophets arrived from Jerusalem. One of them, Agabus, 'showed by the Spirit' that there would be a worldwide famine – which took place in the days of Claudius, emperor from AD 41 to 54 (Acts 11:27–28).

Later, when Paul and his companions were making their way to Jerusalem, they stayed 'many days' in the port city of Caesarea at the house of Philip the evangelist. While they were there, Agabus, who had prophesied earlier about the famine, took Paul's belt and tied his hands and feet with it. Prophesying, Agabus said the Jews in Jerusalem would bind Paul's hands and feet in the same way, and hand Paul over to the Gentiles. Paul, however, was determined to continue on his way to Jerusalem – where Agabus's prophecy came true.

Teachers

After apostles and prophets come teachers (1 Corinthians 12:28). The Greek word for 'teacher' here refers to 'those who in the religious assemblies of Christians undertake the work of teaching, with the special assistance of the Holy Spirit' (*Thayer's Greek Lexicon*). Teachers, who unfold Scripture, must have an accurate knowledge of God's word, so they can convey its truth correctly to the members of God's flock.

The elders are the shepherds (pastors) of the local church and as such must be able to teach sound doctrine (1 Timothy 3:2), so they can feed the flock with the nourishing words of truth. On his way to Jerusalem Paul calls for the elders of the church in Ephesus and commands them to 'shepherd' the church; that is, protect and feed it (Acts 20:28). The 'overseer/bishop' (elder) must hold fast to 'the faithful word' (Titus 1:9).

Whereas the ministries of the apostle, prophet and evangelist are mobile ministries, the shepherd-teachers are likely based in local churches (Apollos, see below, seems to have been an exception). Sheep need daily access to a shepherd they know well and trust to receive their food and water. It would be unusual for such a shepherd to be travelling regularly to far-flung congregations rather than attending to the 'sheep' in his own town or geographical area.

Apollos

Apollos, the Alexandrian Jew who converted to Christianity, is probably the best-known example of a teacher in the New Testament. We meet him first in Acts 18 when he comes to the synagogue in Ephesus. There Paul's friends Aquila and Priscilla hear him speaking boldly and suggest he go to Greece. He agrees and goes to
Corinth, where he puts his deep knowledge of Scripture to use and greatly helps the believers (Acts 18:24–28; 19:1).

Paul the apostle 'planted' the church in Corinth, and Apollos the teacher 'watered' it (1 Corinthians 3:6). All we know about Apollos was that he was a teacher. Nowhere do we read that the 'signs of an apostle', the holy miraculous, accompanied his ministry.

Evangelists

The office of the evangelist is fourth in the list of church offices Paul speaks of in 1 Corinthians 12:28. The evangelist exercises his ministry outside the church in the highways and byways of the world, where people hear his message of the good news of Jesus. When Jesus said to the Eleven, 'Go into all the world and preach the gospel to every creature,' He might as well have been referring to the evangelist's ministry (Mark 16:15).

Not only does the evangelist preach the gospel, but he also performs miracles of healing and casts out demons. His ministry is accompanied by the spectacular and the holy supernatural. Only one man in the New Testament has the title 'evangelist'.

Philip

Philip is one of the seven deacons appointed along with the first Christian martyr, Stephen (Acts 6:5).

When the storm of persecution breaks out against the Christians in Jerusalem, Philip is one of those who travels to other regions to preach the gospel. Arriving in the city of Samaria, he preaches Christ to them. Multitudes listen to him and see the miracles he does and hear the demons scream out of the demonized people listening to Philip (Acts 8:5–7).

Sometime later an angel tells Philip to go south, into the desert. Being a man of deep faith, Philip obeys and finds an Ethiopian, an official of the Queen of Ethiopia, returning home from Jerusalem. Philip speaks to him, he is converted to Christ and Philip baptizes him. As Philip baptizes him, Philip is caught away and finds himself at the town of Azotus (Ashdod) (Acts 8:26–40).

Was the fourfold ministry meant to pass away?

God's church has apostles, prophets, evangelists and shepherd-teachers, a *fourfold ministry* (compare 1 Corinthians 12:28–29). Paul tells us the purpose of these ministries: (1) 'for the equipping of the saints for the work of ministry', (2) 'for the building up of the body of Christ', so that (3) we may 'come to the unity of the faith' and (4) the unity of 'the knowledge of the Son of God', that (5) we may become 'a perfect man' reaching the stature of 'the fullness of Christ', that (6) we should 'no longer be children' tossed about by various strange doctrines, but may (7) 'grow up in all things' into Christ (Ephesians 4:11–15). The input of the fourfold ministries causes the growth of the church until it reaches maturity and becomes a 'perfect man'.

The English Standard Version adds a subtle new meaning to Ephesians 4:11: 'And he gave *the* apostles, *the* prophets, *the* evangelists, *the* shepherds and teachers' (my emphases), making this verse refer to the ministries *already given* at the time Paul wrote his letter to the Ephesian church, and implying these ministries would not continue! However, the Greek of verse 11 says, literally, 'And he gave *some indeed* apostles, *some now* prophets, *some now* evangelists, *some now* shepherds and teachers' (my emphases). Whoever translated this part of the English Standard Version seems not to have believed the fourfold ministry was meant to last, and introduced his or her own bias into the text. (The popular New International Version translation of Ephesians 4:11 is similar to that of the ESV.)

Now, if these ministries were needed in the early church, for the Christians to become strong and be perfected, would they not also be needed throughout the coming years of church history until Jesus returns? If the way those Christians reached maturity was through the fourfold ministry, how can modern Christians become perfected unless they too receive the fourfold ministry?

So, would, or did, God indeed change His blueprint? Would it not be more likely to be the *devil* who changed the blueprint – to achieve his own sinister ends? When God does something, He does it perfectly the first time – there is no need to make any changes.

5

Disaster in the second century AD

> Diotrephes, who loves to have the *first place* among them. (3 John 9; my emphasis)

John B. Lightfoot, professor of divinity at the University of Cambridge in the late 1800s, said that before the middle of the second century AD every church had *three* ranks of ministers: a 'bishop' (overseer), 'presbyters' (elders) and deacons (*Saint Paul's Epistle to the Philippians*, p. 186). However, as we have seen, the office of bishop (*episkopos*) and elder (*presbyteros*) until around the end of the first century AD had been *identical* – two different words for the same ministry. At the end of the first century, churches had only overseers/elders and deacons, which is shown clearly in the first letter of Clement.

1 Clement

The Christians in Rome wrote this letter to the Christians in Corinth around AD 95–96. G. Davis says this is one of the earliest existing letters we have apart from the New Testament ('The Development of the Canon of the New Testament'). Davis says, although the letter does not name its writer, 'well-attested ancient tradition identifies it as the work of Clement', who might have been an elder in Rome.

Lightfoot, quoting from section 42 of the letter, points out that 1 Clement mentions only two orders of officers in the local church, those of 'bishops' (presbyters/elders) and 'deacons', and says the office of 'bishop' and 'presbyter' is at that stage of church history interchangeable (*Saint Paul's Epistle to the Philippians*, pp. 97–98).

In section 44, 1 Clement uses the terms 'episcopate' (the group of bishops/overseers in the local church) and 'presbyters', again without any distinction between these two groups. However, this synonymous use of 'presbyters', 'elders' and 'bishops' seems not to appear again outside the New Testament in any of the other early Christian writings apart from the *Didache* and Jerome's *Commentary on the Epistle to Titus* (see below).

The *Didache*

The *Didache* (Teaching), a Christian manual, was written sometime between AD 50 and AD 165. In chapter 15 it gives instructions concerning 'bishops and deacons', who also function as 'prophets and teachers'. As in 1 Clement, there is no mention of a 'bishop' versus 'presbyters/elders', which suggests that the writer of the *Didache* saw no distinction between bishops and elders – therefore mirroring the New Testament, where bishops are elders and elders are bishops.

Ignatius of Antioch

The earliest existing Christian writings that separate the office of 'bishop' from that of 'presbyter/elder' are the letters of Ignatius of Antioch, dating from the early second century AD.

K. Lake says the church historian Eusebius of Caesarea (260–339) calls Ignatius the third 'bishop' of Antioch in Syria. However, P. Foster says, 'The consistent testimony of early Christian writing is to describe Ignatius as the second Bishop of Antioch, although there is some confusion surrounding his predecessor' ('The Epistles of Ignatius of Antioch (Part I)', p. 490).

Ignatius was condemned to die in the amphitheatre of Rome by the mouth of savage animals. On his way to the imperial city he passed through churches in Asia Minor (modern-day Turkey), and when in Smyrna wrote to the churches of Ephesus, Magnesia, Tralles and Rome. When he arrived at Troas (Troy) he wrote to the churches of Philadelphia and Smyrna, and to Polycarp, Bishop of Smyrna. Foster says Eusebius records Ignatius's martyrdom as having taken place around AD 110. However, Foster argues, on the basis of their content, that the letters could have been written as late as AD 125–50, thus calling into question the widely accepted date of 110 for Ignatius's martyrdom.

But whether we accept the date of 110 or 125–50, Ignatius's letters are the first examples we have of the shift in leadership in local churches from a group of co-equal elders to one man leading the rest, the 'bishop' who presided over 'elders' with less authority than his.

I have searched through Ignatius's letters and have found many examples of this new church structure he seems to have introduced – a separation of the elders into a bishop and elders. Below are seven examples, taken from J.B. Lightfoot's translation *The Apostolic Fathers* (I have modernized his English and the emphases are mine):

> submitting yourselves to your *bishop* and *presbytery*, you may be sanctified in all things. (*Ephesians* 2)

> he is subject to the *bishop* as to the grace of God and to the *presbytery* as to the law of Jesus Christ. (*Magnesians* 2)

> there is one altar, as there is one *bishop*, together with the *presbytery*. (*Philadelphians* 4)

> the churches which are nearest have sent *bishops*, and others *presbyters*. (*Philadelphians* 10)

Do you all follow your *bishop*, as Jesus Christ followed the Father, and the *presbytery* as the Apostles. (*Smyrnaeans* 8)

I salute your godly *bishop* and your venerable *presbytery*. (*Smyrnaeans* 12)

Give ye heed to the *bishop*, that God also may give heed to you. I am devoted to those who are subject to the *bishop*, the *presbyters*, the deacons. (*Polycarp* 6)

K.S. Latourette writes that in the early part of the second century

we now hear indisputably of what soon came to be the accepted pattern, a bishop governing a particular church and of at least one bishop [Ignatius], that of the church in Antioch, *acting as though it were his acknowledged right to address himself with authority to other churches.* (*A History of Christianity, Volume I: to A.D. 1500*, p. 116; my emphasis)

He says furthermore, 'The emphatic fashion in which he [Ignatius] stressed these officers [the bishops, presbyters and deacons] and respect for them may be evidence that the position which he advocated for them had not yet won general acceptance' (p. 117).

J.B. Lightfoot adds that towards the end of the second century 'the original application of the term "bishop" seems to have passed not only out of use, but almost out of memory' (*Saint Paul's Epistle to the Philippians*, p. 98).

Reed Merino helpfully pointed out to me that Ignatius supposedly wrote thirteen letters. But scholars have reduced this number to seven. And another important point Reed mentioned was as follows.

Ignatius strongly insists on there being a 'bishop' (*episkopos*) ruling a congregation, distinguishing this office from that of the elder/presbyter. However, Ignatius makes no mention of such a 'bishop' ruling the church in *Rome*. In his letter to Rome, Ignatius uses *episkopos* twice only, both times referring to himself. He writes of himself as the 'bishop of Syria'. Had there been a ruling bishop in Rome at that time, surely Ignatius would have mentioned him – in the way he mentioned ruling bishops in his other letters. So, as there seems to have been no ruling bishop in the important Roman church early in the second century, this office was added at some point after Ignatius wrote to the church there. Indeed, had Ignatius mentioned a ruling bishop to the Roman church, which did not yet have such an office, what he was describing would have sounded foreign to them.

Many second-century AD bishops

To try to build his case for the acceptability of the office of ruling bishop, Lightfoot gives the names of many second-century AD bishops. For example, Ignatius, Hero, Theophilus and Serapion of Antioch, Polycarp of Smyrna, Onesimus and Polycrates of Ephesus (*The Christian Ministry*, pp. 54–55, 57). *Could it be that all these based their new office on the letters of Ignatius?*

The apostle John

Lightfoot says Asia Minor, where the apostle John and other apostles lived after Jerusalem's fall in AD 70, 'was the nurse, if not the mother, of episcopacy in the Gentile churches' (*The Christian Ministry*, p. 48). Lightfoot adds that the important institution of episcopacy 'developed in a Christian community of which St. John was the living centre and guide' and 'could hardly have grown up without his sanction' (p. 48).

Jerome's conflicting views on bishops

Jerome (born around 347, died 419/429), the leading biblical scholar in the late fourth and early fifth century AD, is perhaps best known for his translation of the Bible into Latin, the so-called Vulgate (from the Latin *editio vulgata,* 'common version').

He wrote many works, which had a great impact on the later history of the church. Among them was his *Commentary on the Epistle to Titus* (around AD 387), in which he writes (emphases mine):

> A presbyter, therefore, is *the same as a bishop*, and before dissensions were introduced into religion by the instigation of the devil, and it was said among the peoples, 'I am of Paul, I am of Apollos, and I of Cephas,' *Churches were governed by a common council of presbyters*; afterwards, when everyone thought that those whom he had baptised were his own, and not Christ's, it was decreed in the whole world that one chosen out of the presbyters should be placed over the rest, and to whom all care of the Church should belong, that the seeds of schisms might be plucked up. Whosoever thinks that there is no proof from Scripture, but that this is my opinion, that a *presbyter and bishop are the same*, and that one is a title of age, the other of office, let him read the words of the apostle to the Philippians, saying, 'Paul and Timotheus, servants of Christ to all the saints in Christ Jesus which are at Philippi with the *bishops and deacons.*'

And then:

Therefore, as we have shown, among the ancients *presbyters were the same as bishops*; but by degrees, that the plants of dissension might be rooted up, all responsibility was transferred to one person. Therefore, as the presbyters know that it is by the custom of the Church that they are to be subject to him who is placed over them so let the bishops know that they are above presbyters rather *by custom than by Divine appointment*, and ought to rule the Church *in common*, following the example of Moses, who, when he alone had power to preside over the people Israel, chose seventy, with the assistance of whom he might judge the people. We see therefore what kind of presbyter or bishop should be ordained.

(Translated from Patrologia latina 26:562–563, and mentioned in Brand and Norman [eds], *Perspectives on Church Government*. My thanks first to Reed K. Merino, and then to Ken Temple, *Apologetics and Agape* blog, for this info.)

However, in his work *On Illustrious Men* (392/393), Jerome backtracks on what he wrote around five years earlier in his *Commentary on the Epistle to Titus* (my emphases):

Polycarp disciple of the apostle John and by him *ordained bishop of Smyrna* was *chief* of all Asia, where he saw and had as teachers some of the apostles and of those who had seen the Lord.

He, on account of certain questions concerning the day of the Passover, went to Rome in the time of the emperor Antoninus Pius while Anicetus *ruled the church* in that city. (Chapter 17)

This is curious – why do such an abrupt about turn? Reed Merino offers this explanation. He thinks Jerome was going along with the general trend in church history where those steering the ship believed God was in the business of 'improving' His church. A kind of doctrinal evolutionism.

It is human nature to want to be at the head of the queue, to be superior to others – in the way Lucifer was unhappy about where he was in God's hierarchy. He wanted the top position, *to be God*. This new teaching about the one-man-in-charge rulership of the church, of being a 'monarchical bishop', fell right in line with human ambition and quickly became the norm in the church.

The statements of Irenaeus, Clement of Alexandria and Tertullian on bishops

Irenaeus (131–201), Bishop of Lyons, in his *Against Heresies* says the following (my emphases):

we are in a position to reckon up those who were by the apostles instituted bishops in the Churches, and [to demonstrate] the *succession of these men* to our own times. (3.3.1)

The blessed apostles [Peter and Paul], then, having founded and built up the Church [at Rome], committed into the hands of Linus the *office of the episcopate.* (3.3.3)

Polycarp . . . was also, by apostles in Asia, appointed *bishop of the Church in Smyrna*, whom I also saw in my early youth. (3.3.4)

Irenaeus seems to be the first second-century writer who says apostles appointed 'bishops'.

Towards the end of the second century or in the early third century Clement of Alexandria in North Africa (150–215), in his treatise *Who Is the Rich Man That Shall Be Saved?*, says when the apostle John

returned to Ephesus from the isle of Patmos, he went away, being invited, to the contiguous territories of the nations, here to *appoint bishops*, there to set in order whole Churches, there to ordain such as were marked out by the Spirit. (Section 42; my emphasis)

Tertullian (160–240), from Carthage in North Africa, adds, 'The sequence of bishops traced back to its origin will be found to rest on the authority of John' (quoted in Lightfoot, *The Christian Ministry*, p. 56).

In the last half of the second century, around fifty years after the apostle John died, we have Irenaeus saying 'apostles instituted bishops'. He does not mention John by name, although he perhaps implies John was one of these apostles.

So, the first *mention* of apostles appointing bishops appears fifty years after this is supposed to have happened. Could it be that Clement of Alexandria, Tertullian and Jerome based their comments on those of Irenaeus? We know this is common in history – a respected writer makes a statement that, although false, other writers then repeat and add to, until a legend forms and the original, false, statement becomes widely accepted as gospel truth. The 'doctrinal evolutionism' mentioned above.

As Reed Merino says (personal communication):

> One might also add that the earliest testimonies about the 'episcopacy/presbytery' (the Scriptures, *Didache* and 1 Clement) all clearly describe them as members of a *team* of leaders. It is only the later writers who speak of a single 'bishop'. That in itself is evidence to

prove that we are talking about a subsequent development into the hierarchical version.

How reliable are Irenaeus's writings?

On the Alpha and Omega Ministries website, in the article 'Irenaeus and the Reliability of "Early" Oral Tradition', the writer says that

> just because Irenaeus declares something to be tradition and is one of the earliest fathers (though not one of the apostolic fathers), it does not mean that Irenaeus got it right. Sometimes . . . Irenaeus got it horribly wrong.

The writer gives two examples of serious error from Irenaeus. The first is Irenaeus's statement that Jesus died at around *fifty* years of age (*Against Heresies* 2.22.5). We know, however, that Jesus died around the age of *thirty* – twenty years lower than the figure Irenaeus gives (see Luke 3:23).

The second error is that Peter and Paul founded the church at Rome. However, from the contents of Paul's letter to the Romans (15:19–22) it is obvious that Paul was not a founder of the Roman church – he did not arrive in Rome until near the end of his life, four years after around

AD 56, when he wrote his letter to the Romans, most likely from Corinth.

D.W. O'Connor in his article 'St. Peter the Apostle' in the *Encyclopaedia Britannica* states, 'The claims that the church of Rome was founded by Peter or that he served as its first bishop are in dispute and rest on evidence that is not earlier than the middle or late 2nd century.'

As Irenaeus is wrong concerning both historical facts mentioned above, could he be wrong about apostles appointing bishops? The answer has to be yes – we cannot regard Irenaeus as a reliable witness.

And what of Irenaeus's belief (Reed Merino points out) that the phoenix bird reincarnated every 500 years?!

The silence of Ignatius

There is no mention of the apostle John in any of the seven letters of Ignatius. If John appointed bishops as a separate class to presbyters/elders, why is Ignatius silent on this? It would greatly have strengthened Ignatius's repeated focus on the priority of the bishop had he been able to point to John as the authority for the office of bishop. *Ignatius's silence is deafening and is a strong argument against John's appointing bishops.*

Could it be that John appointed *elders* in various churches – as Luke tells us Paul and Barnabas had done many years before (Acts 14:23)? And that the report of these appointments somehow later changed into John's ordaining one-man ruling 'bishops'? We do not know, as our sources of information from those distant days are scarce.

Did John ordain bishops?

If we take the author of 3 John to be the apostle John (see the letter of Jerome to Evangelus, in which Jerome states that John wrote 3 John), John mentions a certain Diotrephes. Diotrephes seems to be an elder in the church to whom the apostle writes, a man 'who loves to have the first place among them' (verse 9), who acts in a dictatorial way in the church. The Greek word used here for 'first place' means 'fond of being first' or 'to strive to be first' (*Thayer's Greek Lexicon*), and is used only here in the New Testament.

It is clear in this letter that John does not approve of one elder acting independently of the other elders – Gaius also seems to be one of the elders of the church (verse 1). John praises Demetrius and may be hinting it would be better if he were to replace the self-promoting Diotrephes (verse 12). The idea of a 'bishop' versus elders/presbyters is absent from this short letter.

Are we really to believe John took it upon himself to change the blueprint laid out in the New Testament – of a team of co-equal elders, rather than a single 'bishop', overseeing local churches? Would he have replaced the office of an apostle with that of a 'bishop'?

As we saw earlier, 'bishop', which means 'overseer', is just another term for an 'elder' and 'shepherd' – words that describe different functions of the same office. One man combines in himself the office of overseer, elder and shepherd, and this man in the New Testament is *always* a co-equal part of a male leadership *team* (usually described as 'elders'). The modern church structure, with, say, a 'pastor' (male or female) at the helm, or a 'bishop' (male or female) over a 'diocese', clashes with the simple leadership structure in the New Testament.

Is it reasonable to assume the Lord altered the leadership structure of His church just before the death of the apostle John, the last of the Twelve? There is no hint anywhere in the New Testament that a new, one-man, leadership role was meant to replace the eldership.

Why did ancient writers say John appointed bishops?

This perplexing question has at least three possible answers: (1) John really did ordain bishops, or (2) those who claimed John made such appointments based their statements on those of earlier writers, without checking to see if these writers had their facts straight, or (3) these early voices lied.

Regarding point 1, as we saw in the section above, it is unlikely John would so radically have changed the blueprint for local church leadership, which would have undermined the foundation carefully laid by, for example, the apostle Paul. A thorough search for the word 'elder' (singular) in the book of Acts turns up no examples. However, 'elders' (plural) appears nineteen times (4:5, 8, 23; 5:21; 6:12; 11:30; 14:23; 15:2, 4, 6, 22, 23; 16:4; 20:17; 21:18; 22:5; 23:14; 24:1; 25:15). 'Bishop' (overseer) appears just three times in the New Testament, always as 'a bishop' and never as '*the* bishop' (1 Timothy 3:1, 2; Titus 1:7), whereas 'bishops' (plural) appears once (Philippians 1:1).

Furthermore, Paul says the *presbyterion*, the body or council of elders, laid hands on Timothy (1 Timothy 4:14). This probably took place when Timothy left the city of Lystra to join Paul and Silas on their apostolic journey (Acts 14:21–23; 16:1–3).

Regarding point 2, it is human nature to accept the statements of respected people as truth. Ignatius had the title 'Bishop of Antioch', wrote seven letters to various churches and was later a martyr. Many who read his letters would have had held him in awe, so, when he wrote repeatedly of respecting the 'bishop' of a church, and separates the 'bishop' from the 'elders' (presbyters), these readers would likely have gone along with him without asking too many questions. After all, he was a 'bishop' and a seemingly godly, man on his way to martyrdom. What he said in his letters must have been true would have been the reasoning.

Irenaeus too was the 'Bishop of Lyons' and his *Against Heresies* was no doubt respected by the Christians of his day. Moreover, he had personally heard the saintly Polycarp, who was also later martyred. People would suppose that if Irenaeus said the apostle John appointed Polycarp as the Bishop of Smyrna, then this appointment must indeed have happened.

Church 'father' thus built on the writings of other church 'fathers', so that by the end of the second century the system of a 'bishop' assisted by 'presbyters' had become the norm.

Something else to keep in mind is human pride. Many people love having a title and being elevated above others. It was prestigious to be the 'bishop' of a city and to be titled 'Bishop' so and so. Jesus' warning in Matthew's Gospel was soon forgotten, 'But you, *do not be called "Rabbi"*; for One is your Teacher, the Christ, and you are all brothers. *Do not call anyone on earth your father*; for One is your Father, He who is in heaven' (23:8–9).

With a title comes power over others, for those people look up to the titled person as an authority figure. And it is human nature to submit blindly to those who are seen as superior or as experts – especially if they have a charismatic personality. However, Lord Acton, in his letter to Bishop Creighton, said memorably, 'Power tends to corrupt and absolute power corrupts absolutely. Great men are almost always bad men, even when they exercise influence and not authority.'

Ignatius, Bishop of Antioch, poured poison into the long river of church history near its source. It seems many paid more attention to his seven letters than to Scripture! As he was on his way to martyrdom and bore the title 'bishop', many Christians seem to have blindly accepted his strange teaching on the importance of the bishop versus a team of co-equal elders. And so, a new, hierarchical church structure was born and began to grow. Satan had scored a *huge* victory. With this new hierarchy came a separation of the congregation into 'clergy' and 'laity'.

Clergy versus laity

Agreeing with J.B. Lightfoot's view on the introduction of a ruling bishop, P. Schaff says there was a need for the church to be more organized than it had been in the first century. With the lessening of spiritual gifts, the system of *clergy* versus *laity* developed. In earlier times, the norm *each time the church assembled* was that any member of the congregation could prophesy, for example, or speak out loudly in tongues, which another member would inter-pret – all the members were equal. But with the emergence of the 'bishop', the focus began to be on his steering the congregation while the other members were less spiritually active than before. *Congregational passivity became the standard.*

The Old Testament's Levitical priesthood, with its high priest, priests and Levites, transferred naturally to the office of bishop, priest and deacon. Whereas before, the local church consisted of the priesthood of all believers, from Ignatius onwards the bishop emerged as supreme (P. Schaff, *History of the Christian Church*, vol. 2, pp. 116–119).

Was James a bishop?

Lightfoot says the Jerusalem church 'presents the earliest instance of a bishop. A certain prominence is assigned to James the Lord's brother' (*The Christian Ministry*, p. 50). He says that as early as AD 150 'all parties concur in representing him as a bishop in the strict sense of the term' (p. 51). But does *Scripture* agree that James was a bishop?

Acts mentions James three times, but never links his name to the office of a bishop (12:17; 15:13; 21:18). In 1 Corinthians 15:7 Paul says James and then 'all the apostles' saw Jesus after His resurrection. This text implies that James too was an apostle. E.D. Burton agrees, speaking of 'Paul's inclusion of James among the apostles (Gal 1:19)' (*The Office of Apostle in the Early Church*, p. 570). Writing to the Galatian churches, Paul says he 'saw none of the *other apostles* except James, the Lord's brother' (a different

'James' from the son of Zebedee, who had been martyred before this time) and that 'James, Cephas [Peter], and John . . . seemed to be pillars' (Galatians 1:19; 2:9). Paul places James on the same level as the apostles John and Peter, and mentions James first in the list.

Could James have been both an apostle and an elder? Yes, for the apostle Peter describes himself as an 'elder' in 1 Peter 5:1. But nowhere in God's word is James called a 'bishop' in Lightfoot's sense of one man in charge of a church, and later a group of churches based in an area.

Trying to justify the abnormal

When reading Lightfoot's *The Christian Ministry*, we must keep in mind that he was a member of the Church of England, which has an established system of 'priests', 'bishops', an 'archbishop', and so on. Also, the year *The Christian Ministry* was published, 1878, is the very year Lightfoot was 'enthroned' as the Bishop of Durham. In *The Christian Ministry* he seems to take great pains to justify the leadership structure of the Church of England that existed then and still exists today.

Lightfoot writes of two stages in the 'progress and operation of the Church' (p. 12) – an earlier stage when the miraculous was evident, and a later stage when the permanent ministry gradually emerged, as the Church assumed a more settled form, and the higher but *temporary* offices, such as the apostolate, fell away. This *progressive* growth and development of the ministry, until it arrived at its *mature and normal* state, it will be the object of the following pages to trace. (P. 14; my emphases)

But was the apostolate 'temporary' and thus meant to fall away? Yes, if we believe the Twelve and Paul were the only apostles – a belief that stands on a foundation of sand, as I have proved above. Was the replacement of the apostolic ministry with that of a 'bishop' a 'mature and normal state'?

Lightfoot says:

History seems to show decisively, that before the middle of the second century each church or organized Christian community had its three orders of minister – its bishop, its presbyters, and its deacons. On this point there cannot reasonably be two opinions. But at what time and under what circumstances this organization was matured, and to what extent *our allegiance is due to it as an authoritative ordinance*, are more difficult questions. Some have recognized in episcopacy an institution of divine origin, absolute and indispensable; others [such as the writer of this book] have represented it as destitute of all apostolic sanction and authority. (*The Christian Ministry*, pp. 15–16; my emphasis)

Jesus says a tree will be known by its fruit. Did the new episcopal system Ignatius of Antioch birthed and promoted so vigorously yield good fruit from the early second century onwards?

In the next chapter we look briefly at what happened to the church in the third and fourth centuries AD, the results of the replacement of the apostle with a 'bishop', a ministry that *had not existed before the early second century*. Contra Lightfoot, might it not be more accurate to speak of the *regress* rather than the *progress* of the church from the second century AD onwards?

6

False teachings of the third to fourth centuries AD

And their message will spread like cancer.
(2 Timothy 2:17)

I do not want to give the impression in what follows that most of the writings of the early church 'fathers' were in error. This would be ridiculous, as much of what they wrote was excellent and is vital for our understanding of the history of Christian doctrine and of what took place in the church – for example, during the reigns of the different Roman emperors.

My aim here is to mention just a few of their strange teachings that invaded the church in the absence of the guidance of God-ordained apostles.

Tertullian (160–240)

Tertullian, from Carthage in North Africa, became a Christian towards the end of the second century AD. He was a lawyer and a prolific writer. In his treatise *On Baptism* he says the baptismal waters cleanse and prepare the believer for the reception of the Holy Spirit. So far so good – what Tertullian says matches Scripture.

But in his next section, on the 'unction', he says when the believer rises out of the baptismal waters he or she is anointed on the body with oil (probably olive oil), followed by the laying on of hands to receive the Spirit.

However, nowhere in the New Testament were believers anointed with oil before being prayed for to receive the Holy Spirit!

Tertullian says the 'chief priest', the bishop, is the one who should administer baptism. Or 'in the next place, the presbyters and deacons, yet not without the bishop's authority' (ch. 17). So, Tertullian too separates the office of bishop from that of presbyter (elder), with the bishop having greater authority than the presbyter.

In this section Tertullian also speaks of 'laymen', and calls the bishop, presbyters and deacons the laymen's 'superiors'. Tertullian thus teaches the heresy of 'clergy' versus 'laity', which flies in the face of the apostle Peter's teaching of the priesthood of all believers (1 Peter 2:5, 9).

Origen (185–254)

Origen, whom church historian Henry Chadwick describes as 'the most important theologian and biblical scholar of the early Greek church', lived in Alexandria, Egypt. Here he became the head of the Catechetical School, which prepared catechumens (new, unbaptized Christians) for water baptism and confirmation.

Among Origen's many false teachings were that Jesus was a created being, the pre-existence of souls, the denial of eternal punishment, and the belief that all – *including Satan* – will eventually be reconciled to God! Origen writes, 'We think that the goodness of God, through the mediation of Christ, will bring all creatures to one and the same end' (*First Principles* 1.6.1–3). The fire of God, says Origen, is for the purification of souls, not for eternal judgement.

Jerry Walls writes of Origen, 'In his Christology, Jesus' soul was one of the souls originally created by God. It did not fall with the others, and was therefore chosen to be united to the divine Logos' ('Universalism in Origen's First Principles', p. 10). Some of these created souls fell to become angels, others, men, and others, demons.

The well-known theologian and scholar Professor William Barclay, himself a universalist (someone who believes all humans will finally be saved), writes in his autobiography:

Origen believed that after death there were many who would need prolonged instruction, the sternest discipline, even the severest punishment before they were fit for the presence of God. Origen did not eliminate hell; he believed that some people would have to go to heaven via hell. He believed that even at the end of the day there would be some on whom the scars remained. He did not believe in eternal punishment, but he did see the possibility of eternal penalty. And so the choice is whether we accept God's offer and invitation willingly, or take the long and terrible way round through ages of purification. (*A Spiritual Autobiography*, p. 665)

What would the apostles have thought of Origen's strange teachings?

Cyprian (200–258)

Converted from paganism, Cyprian received Christian baptism in 245 or 246. Despite his recent conversion, astonishingly, he became the Bishop of Carthage in 248 or 249.

Cyprian believed the episcopate replaced the Jewish priesthood and uses the word 'priest' for the office of bishop throughout his letters. However, around 200 years earlier the apostle Peter, as mentioned above, had written that *all Christians* are a 'holy' and 'royal priesthood' (1 Peter 2:5, 9) – the concept of one man being 'priest' in the congregation was unknown in New Testament times.

For Cyprian the line of bishops stretched back to the time of the apostles, who had appointed the first bishops. At this appointment the apostles had bestowed the Holy

Spirit, who in turn was passed on to subsequent bishops ordained by other bishops. This came to be known as the 'apostolic succession' and bishops were thus carriers of the Holy Spirit.

Cyprian also said that anyone who opposed the bishop was not a part of the church, as the bishop represented the church. And anyone not in the church was unsaved.

Ambrose (339–397)

Ambrose was born in Gaul but grew up in Rome, where his sister was a nun. In around 370 he became the governor of Aemilia-Liguria and lived in Milan. When the bishop died, Ambrose went to a meeting that would decide on the late bishop's replacement. To his amazement those present called for the popular Ambrose to become the new bishop, an office he did not want to take up. Eventually, after a period under arrest, Ambrose caved in and accepted the bishopric.

The amazing thing was that he had not yet been baptized and was still a layman. Usually a presbyter was nominated by the other presbyters in a town to become the bishop. Within eight days of the citizens of Milan clamouring for Ambrose to become the new Bishop of Milan, the unbaptized layman took up his new position in the church.

However, Ambrose's appointment was invalid for at least four reasons: (1) he was inexperienced in Scripture, as he was a recent believer, (2) he had not yet received water baptism (or, presumably, Holy Spirit baptism), (3) the citizens of Carthage – many of whom were most likely not even Christians – were involved in his being ordained a bishop, and (4) the office of 'bishop' in the sense of one man overseeing the churches in a city, as we have seen, is unbiblical.

Central to Ambrose's teaching was that Mary, the mother of Jesus, remained a virgin all her life and, as the 'Mother of God', was sinless, for she never sinned. Ambrose writes:

> What is greater than the Mother of God? What more glorious than she whom Glory Itself chose? What more chaste than she who bore a body without contact with another body? For why should I speak of her other virtues? She was a virgin not only in body but also in mind. (*Concerning Virginity*, 2.2.7)

This laid the groundwork for Mary's later being raised to the status of a goddess in the Roman Catholic system, so she came to be known as Co-Redeemer with Jesus, and the mediator between humans and Him. Ambrose's teaching on Mary influenced the popes Damasus, Siricius and Leo XIII.

The worship of martyrs and relics

Severe persecution of the Christians between the second and fourth centuries AD took place under the Roman emperors Marcus Aurelius (161–80), Decius and Valerian (249–60) and Diocletian (303–11). These persecutions resulted in the deaths of multitudes of Christians, who came to be known as 'martyrs' – people killed for holding a certain belief.

Historian Philip Schaff says the day on which a martyr died was known as his or her heavenly birthday. This was celebrated each year at the place where the martyr was buried. Schaff continues:

Martyrdom was taken, after the end of the second century, not only as a higher grade of Christian virtue, but at the same time as a baptism of fire and blood, an ample substitution for the baptism of water, as purifying from sin, and as securing an entrance into heaven. Origen even went so far as to ascribe to the sufferings of the martyrs an atoning virtue for others, an efficacy like that of the sufferings of Christ . . . According to Tertullian, the martyrs entered immediately into the blessedness of heaven, and were not required, like ordinary Christians, to pass through the intermediate state. (*History of the Christian Church*, vol. 2, p. 85).

Not only were the martyrs themselves honoured, but so were their possessions and bones, their so-called 'relics'. Schaff relates that when Cyprian died the martyr's death, his friends gathered his blood in handkerchiefs and later built a chapel over his tomb (p. 86).

Conclusion

Look, all you who kindle a fire,
Who encircle yourselves with sparks:
Walk in the light of your fire and in the sparks you
have kindled . . .
(Isaiah 50:11)

Strange teachings crept from church to church in the third and fourth centuries AD. The office of bishop was now well established and the structure of the church had changed dramatically from the one laid out in the New Testament. By the end of the first century AD, the church still held to the 'faith which was once for all delivered to the holy ones' (Jude 3), but from the second century onwards the waters rapidly became muddier.

The cause of this pollution was in large part due to the pronouncements of famous 'bishops', now known as church 'fathers', who had *replaced* the apostles and brought many heretical teachings into the church. The writings of these 'fathers', also known as 'tradition', to a great extent began to take the place of Scripture and, with each passing generation, these men introduced more error.

The apostle Paul, probably around the early 60s AD, warned the Ephesian elders that after his departure 'savage wolves will come in among you, not sparing the flock', and that 'from among yourselves men will rise up, speaking perverse things, to draw away the disciples after themselves' (Acts 20:29–30). With Paul out of the way there was no longer a strong apostolic hand to (1) prevent ambitious men from seizing power in the churches he had overseen, as Diotrephes would later try to do in one of the churches the apostle John wrote to (3 John 9–11), and (2) keep the doctrinal waters crystal clean, in alignment only with what Jesus and the apostles had taught.

The devil knew in order to succeed in his mission to derail the church he had to get rid of the office of the apostle. The evil one achieved this by replacing the apostolic ministry with the new office of 'bishop' and with men who loved titles, positions of authority in the church, wealth – and living in a palace . . . Tragically, *this situation still exists in some denominations*.

Although in the twentieth century, for example, there were men with genuine apostolic ministries, such as W.F.P. Burton, who served in the Congo, in whose ministry the 'signs of an apostle' were evident, in the main the apostolic ministry had been snuffed out and replaced with offices such as, for example, that of 'moderator', 'general', 'archbishop', 'cardinal', 'metropolitan' or 'pope' – *none of which appears anywhere in the New Testament*.

The devil has schemed and worked hard throughout church history to alter the blueprint God laid out for His church. Satan knows that without the *whole* of the New Testament's fourfold ministry of apostles, prophets, evangelists and shepherd-teachers, it is impossible for Christians to be equipped for the work of ministry, to be built up spiritually until they 'come to the unity of the faith and of the knowledge of the Son of God, to a perfect man, to the measure of the stature of the fullness of Christ'. *Such Christians will never mature spiritually or pose a threat to the evil one*, but will remain 'children', forever 'tossed to and fro and carried about with every wind of doctrine, by the trickery of men, in the cunning craftiness of deceitful plotting' (Ephesians 4:11–14).

Satan knew if he could change the structure of the church and the way it functioned, the Holy Spirit would depart – the holy supernatural would cease, as the church, once made up of 'living stones', would no longer be God's house, and *would no longer threaten Satan's plans*. As recorded in the book of Exodus, Yahweh gave Moses detailed instructions on how the tabernacle – the tent of God's presence – had to be built. Moses received precise details on the colours and materials of the hangings of the tabernacle, the measurements of the various articles of furniture, what these should be made of and where in the tabernacle they should be. Moses carried out his orders to the letter (Exodus 40:16), and what was the result? 'Then the cloud covered the tabernacle of meeting, and the glory of Yahweh filled the tabernacle' (Exodus 40:34). Yahweh's 'glory', the Holy Spirit, will fill only that which conforms to God's specifications. Would God's glory have filled the tabernacle had Moses made part of it the way *he* wanted it to be? Absolutely not.

God's church is a dynamic, living body of Spirit-baptized believers who *each* have a role to play when the church assembles. Paul writes to the church in Corinth, 'How is it then, brothers? *Whenever* you come together, *each of you* has a psalm, has a teaching, has a tongue, has a revelation, has an interpretation. Let all things be done for building up' (1 Corinthians 14:26; my emphases). The focus in an early church meeting was not on the 'pastor', 'vicar', 'minister', and so on, standing behind a pulpit and preaching a sermon, with the congregation just listening. Nor was the focus on entertainment from a loud 'worship band' singing repetitive me-centred songs and performing like a worldly rock group . . .

Body ministry was the norm in the early church's meetings, but with the disappearance of the apostolic ministry (1) the holy supernatural began to ebb away, (2) new hierarchical leadership structures rose up, separating 'clergy' from 'laity' and (3) liturgy replaced the holy spontaneity that had been a vital part of the early church's Spirit-guided meetings. Tragically, *Satan, by the fourth century AD, had largely replaced the New Testament church with his own counterfeit system.*

In this book I have attempted – from Scripture – to show that the ministry of the apostle was meant to continue into the second century and right up to the present. *Had the apostolic ministry continued, church history would have been very different from what has unfolded over the last two thousand years*, and the modern church would be a blazing city on a hill – illuminating the world – instead of the haunted ruin we largely see in the West today.

> The grass withers, the flower fades,
> But the word of our God stands for ever.
> (Isaiah 40:8)

Epilogue

Preach the word! Be ready in season and out of season. Convince, rebuke, exhort, with all longsuffering and teaching. (2 Timothy 4:2)

At the time of writing, June 2024, around a quarter of the twenty-first century has slipped into history. Denominations – each following its own religious formula – have mushroomed throughout the world, and most are steered by a 'pastor', 'senior pastor', husband and wife 'pastors', a 'lead elder' or 'minister'. These people often do a correspondence course or attend a Bible college or seminary for a number of years and then receive a piece of paper that – in the eyes of their denomination and its followers – qualifies them for spiritual leadership. But where do we find this system in the Bible?

As mentioned above, in the non-negotiable New Testament blueprint elders/overseers/shepherds (always plural) were ordained by an apostle (Acts 14:23; Titus 1:5). So, should we assemble with a church that has leadership not ordained in the New Testament way? If the captain of a ship is unfamiliar with sea maps that show reefs and sea depths, is not properly qualified to steer that ship and does not know how to deal with strong winds and high waves, *what will happen to his ship and the people on board when they face a severe storm or hit the rocks*? Will the passengers who entrusted their lives – and money – to their captain stay safe?

In my opinion, it is foolish to think that by staying within a denominational church a believer can somehow change that system so it conforms to the New Testament pattern of 'doing church'. Once a wrong foundation is in place and a house is built on it, it is pointless trying to pull the walls down or to dig up and relay the foundation. People believe what they want to believe and find comfort in the familiar. They do not like to have their boat rocked. So, the wisest option is simply to leave the doomed ship before it sinks – and find safety in a godly house church. The words of Joshua come to mind:

> And if it seems evil to you to serve Yahweh, choose for yourselves this day whom you will serve, whether the gods which your fathers served that were on the other side of the River, or the gods of the Amorites, in whose land you dwell. But as for me and my house, we will serve Yahweh. (Joshua 24:15)

And the apostle Paul says, 'God, who made the world and everything in it, since He is Lord of heaven and earth, *does not dwell in temples made with hands*' (Acts 17:24; my emphasis). A building with a sign outside naming such and such a 'church' and a board giving the name of the 'minister' or 'pastor' and his (or her) academic qualifications should be a red flag to any Spirit-baptized believer keen to follow the New Testament blueprint.

To avoid compromise, true disciples of Jesus should avoid the denominational ships plying the world's oceans. Instead, they should assemble together in each other's homes, as the first followers of Jesus did. He says, 'For where two or three are gathered together *in My name*, I am there in the midst of them' (Matthew 18:20; my emphasis). Meeting like this to care for one another, study the Bible and pray together – under the direction of the Holy Spirit – is the safest way not to be taken captive (brainwashed) by the false teachings, 'doctrines of demons', that abound in every man-made denomination.

Each believer baptized in the Holy Spirit has something to contribute when the body of Christ assembles. To repeat Paul's instructions to the church in Corinth:

How is it then, brothers? Whenever you come together, each of you has a psalm, has a teaching, has a tongue, has a revelation, has an interpretation. Let all things be done for building up. (1 Corinthians 14:26)

This type of meeting has no 'Pastor' so and so, no pulpit personality, who loves to lord it over the assembled flock of God. Or someone using the church as a *business* so he can make money and have a title people look up to. No – all those who assemble must do so in humility, thinking the others better than themselves and being submitted to the leading of the Holy Spirit in the fear of God.

A word of personal testimony.

In the 1970s when I was a young university student, I attended a church in a place that will remain nameless. The meetings operated following the 1 Corinthians 14:26 format. The church had a number of male elders – it was not steered by one man. Each Sunday morning there was a 'breaking of bread' service that ran from about 10.30 to 12 noon. The elders took it in turns to preside over these services to ensure godly order was kept.

We all sat in a large circle, with the unleavened bread and grape juice on a table in the centre. The service began with singing hymns chosen spontaneously by various members, male or female – accompanied by a skilled pianist, who was a lecturer in the university's music department. There was no hymn list to work through.

Gradually a theme would develop, say on God's holiness.

The hymn-singing was followed by a time of prayer, the ladies wearing head coverings, as God's apostle stipulates in 1 Corinthians 11:5–10. During this time of prayer there was open ministry when any of the members could contribute, for example, Spirit-inspired tongues followed by a Spirit-inspired interpretation. Some members might utter Spirit-inspired prophecies, while others might read a portion of Scripture – say one of the psalms. Or someone else might start to sing a chorus or hymn, while the rest of us gladly joined in.

The theme the Holy Spirit brought into the meeting would develop, for the Spirit, not a human, steered the meeting's direction and there was a strong sense of God's presence.

We all knew, from the Spirit, when the time of prayer was meant to end – it was not humanly controlled. The breaking of bread followed.

After we'd all partaken of a piece of unleavened cracker and grape juice, the presiding elder would say something like, 'Do any of the brothers have something from the Lord to share with us?' (In line with 1 Timothy 2:9–11, the ladies were not allowed to teach doctrine in the assembly, although they could pray and prophesy – providing their heads were covered.) Various male believers would give a 5–10-minute message, and the meeting's theme would continue. The meeting would end with a closing hymn, again chosen spontaneously by one of the members, male or female.

When we left, we knew we had met with God and had heard the message He wanted us to hear. We had not sat for an hour listening to a sermon from a 'pastor' . . .

Sadly, since the 1970s, *on three continents*, I have rarely been in another meeting like those, even though open ministry is how *every* Christian gathering should function.

About the author

Based in the UK, Eldo Barkhuizen has worked as a freelance copy editor and proofreader in the field of Christian and general non-fiction publishing for 27 years.

He has a BA in church history and has copyedited and proofread books on church history, theology and biblical studies for publishers such as Zondervan, HarperCollins, Routledge, Inter-Varsity Press, SPCK, Sheffield Academic Press, Paternoster Press and Hodder & Stoughton among others. See his website at **www.arroweditorial.com**.

His passion is to see the church regain its former glory. But this will happen only if it returns to the 'old paths' the prophet Jeremiah describes (6:16):

> Thus says Yahweh:
>   'Stand in the ways and see,
>   And ask for the old paths,
>   where the good way is,
>   And walk in it;
>   Then you will find rest for your souls.'

Select bibliography

#101: *The Didache* <https://christianhistoryinstitute.org/study/module/didache>, accessed 21 June 2021.

Addison, S.B., 'A Basis for the Continuing Ministry of the Apostle in the Church's Mission', DMin thesis, Fuller Theological Seminary, 1995.

'A Female Apostle?' <https://cbmw.org/2007/06/26/a-female-apostle/>, accessed 24 May 2021.

Barclay, W., *A Spiritual Autobiography* (Grand Rapids: Eerdmans, 1977).

Beard, M., *The Roman Triumph* (Cambridge, Mass.: Harvard University Press, 2007).

Bradshaw, R., 'Ambrose of Milan' <https://earlychurch.org.uk/ambrose.php>, accessed 11 August 2021.

Brand, C.O., and R. S. Norman (eds), *Perspectives on Church Government: Five Views of Church Polity* (Brentwood: Broadman & Holman, 2004), pp. 251–252.

Brown, P.R.L., 'St. Ambrose', *Encyclopaedia Britannica* <https://www.britannica.com/biography/Saint-Ambrose>, accessed 18 August 2021.

Burton, E.D., 'The Office of Apostle in the Early Church', *American Journal of Theology*, vol. 16, no. 4 (October 1912), pp. 561–588.

Busenitz, N., 'Are There Still Apostles Today?' <https://thecripplegate.com/are-there-still-apostles-today>, accessed 20 May 2021.

Cyprian, *The Epistles of Cyprian*, Epistle 1, *To Donatus* <https://www.andrews.edu/~toews/classes/sources/early/Cyprian%20Epistles.htm>, accessed 13 July 2021.

Emmett, D.N., 'W.F.P. Burton (1886–1971) and Congolese Agency: A Biographical Study of a Pentecostal Mission', PhD thesis, University of Birmingham, 2016.

Fellows, R.G., and A.C. Stewart, 'Euodia, Syntyche and the Role of Syzygos: Phil 4:2–3' <https://www.degruyter.com/document/doi/10.1515/znw-2018-0012/html>, accessed 13 May 2021.

Foster, P., 'The Epistles of Ignatius of Antioch (Part I)', *Expository Times*, vol. 117, no. 12 (2006), pp. 487–495.

Giles, K., 'Apostles Before and After Paul', *Churchman*, vol. 99, no. 3 (1985), pp. 241–256.

Harris III, W.H., '1. The Authorship of 1 John' <https://bible.org/seriespage/1-authorship-1-john>, accessed 10 June 2021.

Hartmann, A., 'Junia – A Woman Lost in Translation: The Name IOYNIAN in Romans 16:7 and Its History of Interpretation', De Gruyter, published online 19 November 2020 <https://doi.org/10.1515/opth-2020-0138>, accessed 24 May 2021.

Hatch, E., *The Organization of the Early Christian Churches: Eight Lectures* (Rivingtons: London, 1881).

Hort, F.J.A., 'Lightfoot, Joseph Barber', *Dictionary of National Biography*, 1885–1900, vol. 33 <https://en.wikisource.org/wiki/Dictionary_of_National_

Biography,_1885-1900/Lightfoot,_Joseph_Barber>, accessed 18 August 2021.

Huttar, D., 'Did Paul Call Andronicus an Apostle in Romans 16:7?', *Journal of the Evangelical Theological Society* (December 2009), pp. 747–778.

Irenaeus, *Against Heresies*, Book 1 <https://ccel.org/ccel/ irenaeus/against_heresies_i/anf01>, accessed 18 August 2021.

'Irenaeus and the Reliability of "Early" Oral Tradition' <https://www.aomin.org/aoblog/roman-catholicism/irenaeus-and-the-reliability-of-early-oral-tradition>, accessed 8 July 2021.

Jerome, *On Illustrious Men* <https://www.newadvent.org/ fathers/2708.htm>, accessed 7 July 2021.

Latourette, K.S., *A History of Christianity*, vol. 1: *Beginnings to 1500*, rev. edn (New York: HarperSanFrancisco, 1975).

Lightfoot, J.B., *Epistle to the Philippians*, 4th edn (London: Macmillan, 1878).

Lightfoot, J.B., *St. Paul's Epistle to the Galatians* (Andover: W.F. Draper, 1870).

Lightfoot, J.B., *The Apostolic Fathers* (Grand Rapids: Christian Classics Ethereal Library, no date).

Lightfoot, J.B., *The Christian Ministry* (New York: T. Whittaker, 1878).

Lockyer, H., *All the Women of the Bible* <https://www.

biblegateway.com/resources/all-women-bible/Euodias>, accessed 22 May 2021.

Lockyer, H., *All the Women of the Bible* <https://www.biblegateway.com/resources/all-women-bible/Syntyche>, accessed 22 May 2021.

Miller, D., 'Are There Modern-Day Apostles?', Apologetics Press <https://apologeticspress.org/article/1226>, accessed 20 May 2021.

Moo, D., '9. What Does It Mean Not to Teach or Have Authority Over Men (1 Timothy 2:11–15)' <https://bible.org/seriespage/9-what-does-it-mean-not-teach-or-have-authority-over-men-1-timothy-211-15>, accessed 21 May 2021.

Murphy, S., 'Origen: Heretic or Prophet?' <https://www.researchgate.net/publication/341597654_Origen_Heretic_or_Prophet_Origen_Heretic_or_Prophet>, accessed 10 August 2021.

'Neo-Platonism' <https://www.newadvent.org/cathen/10742b.htm>, accessed 10 August 2021.

O'Connor, D.W., 'St. Peter the Apostle', *Encyclopaedia Britannica* <https://www.britannica.com/biography/Saint-Peter-the-Apostle/Tradition-of-Peter-in-Rome>, accessed 23 August 2021.

'Origen' <https://ccel.org/ccel/origen?queryID=10858935&resultID=380>, accessed 11 August 2021.

'Origen'<https://orthodoxwiki.org/Origen>, accessed 10 August 2021.

'Origen' <https://plato.stanford.edu/entries/origen>, accessed 11 August 2021.

'Origen and Origenism' <https://www.newadvent.org/cathen/11306b.htm>, accessed 11 August 2021.

Pedersen, R., *The Lost Apostle: Searching for the Truth About Junia* (San Francisco: Jossey-Bass, 2006).

Richardson, C.C., 'The Condemnation of Origen', *Church History*, vol. 6, no. 1 (March 1937), pp. 50–64.

Ruthven, J.M., *On the Cessation of the Charismata: The Protestant Polemic on Post-Biblical Miracles*, 2nd edn 2008 <https://www.hopefaithprayer.com/books/On-the-Cessation-of-the-Charismata-Ruthven.pdf>, accessed 2 June 2021.

Sanders, E.P., 'St. Paul the Apostle', *Encyclopaedia Britannica* <https://www.britannica.com/biography/Saint-Paul-the-Apostle>, accessed 11 August 2021.

Schaff, P., 'Ambrose: Selected Works and Letters' <https://www.ccel.org/ccel/schaff/npnf210.html>, accessed 11 August 2021.

Schaff, P., 'Fathers of the Third Century: Hippolytus, Cyprian, Caius, Novatian, Appendix' <https://ccel.org/ccel/schaff/anf05/anf05?queryID=10517399&resultID=>, accessed 13 July 2021.

Schaff, P., 'Fathers of the Third Century: Tertullian, Part Fourth; Minucius Felix; Commodian; Origen, Parts First and Second' <https://ccel.org/ccel/schaff/anf04>, accessed 13 July 2021.

Schaff, P., *Schaff-Herzog Encyclopedia of Religious Knowledge*, vol. 5 (Grand Rapids: Christian Classics Ethereal Library, no date).

'Silas, Silvanus', *Holman Bible Dictionary* <https://www.studylight.org/dictionaries/eng/hbd/s/silas-silvanus.html>, accessed 21 May 2021.

Temple, K., *Apologetics and Agape* (blog) <https://apologeticsandagape.wordpress.com/2021/10/17/jerome-presbyters-are-the-same-as-bishops>, accessed 25 March 2024.

Tertullian, *On Baptism* <https://ccel.org/ccel/tertullian/baptism/anf03.vi.iii.html>, accessed 10 August 2021.

Wace, H., *A Dictionary of Christian Biography and Literature to the End of the Sixth Century A.D., with an Account of the Principal Sects and Heresies* (Grand Rapids: Christian Classics Ethereal Library, no date).

Walls, J., 'Universalism in Origen's First Principles', The Asbury Seminarian <https://place.asburyseminary.edu/cgi/viewcontent.cgi?article=1634&context=asburyjournal>, accessed 11 August 2021.

'What Are the Biblical Qualifications for Apostleship?' <https://www.gotquestions.org/apostleship.html>, accessed 9 June 2021.